Contemporary Indian Writers in English

Amitav Ghosh

Works of Amitav Ghosh

Fiction

The Circle of Reason, 1986
The Shadow Lines, 1988
In An Antique Land: History in the Guise of a Traveller's Tale, 1993
The Calcutta Chromosome: A Novel of Fevers, Delirium and Discovery, 1995
The Glass Palace, 2002
The Hungry Tide, 2004

Non-fiction

Dancing in Cambodia, At Large in Burma, 1998
Countdown, 1999
The Imam and the Indian: Prose Pieces, 2002

(Essays and articles by Amitav Ghosh are listed in the bibliography.)

Contemporary Indian Writers in English

Amitav Ghosh
An Introduction

John C. Hawley

DELHI • BANGALORE • MUMBAI • KOLKATA • CHENNAI • HYDERABAD

Published by

Foundation Books Pvt. Ltd.
CAMBRIDGE HOUSE
4381/4, Ansari Road, Daryaganj
New Delhi - 110 002

C-22, C-Block, Brigade M.M., K.R. Road, Jayanagar, **Bangalore** 560 070
Plot No. 80, Service Industries, Shirvane, Sector-1, Nerul, **Navi Mumbai** 400 706
60, Dr. Sundari Mohan Avenue, 1st Floor, **Kolkata** 700 014
21/1 (New No. 49), 1st Floor, Model School Road, Thousand Lights, **Chennai** 600 006
House No.3-5-874/6/4, (Near Apollo Hospital), Hyderguda, **Hyderabad** 500 029

© Foundation Books Pvt. Ltd.
First published 2005

All rights reserved. No reproduction of any part may take place without the written permission of Foundation Books Pvt. Ltd., subject to statutory exception and to the provision of relevant collective licensing agreements.

ISBN 81-7596-259-3 (Paperback)

Typeset by Techastra Solutions Pvt Ltd, Hyderabad

Cover design by Rohit Raj

Published by Manas Saikia for Foundation Books Pvt. Ltd. and printed and bound at Raj Press, R-3 Inderpuri, New Delhi - 110 012

For my mother, Lilian Callaghan Hawley,
who lived her early years in Bannu

Contents

Series Editor's Preface	ix
1. The Writer, his Contexts and his Themes	1
2. A Writer Situated in a History and in a Place: Ghosh's Non-fiction	18
3. A Tale of Two Riots: *The Circle of Reason* and *The Shadow Lines*	46
4. The Ebb and Flow of Peoples across Continents and Generations: *In An Antique Land, The Glass Palace, The Hungry Tide*	83
5. Subaltern Agency as Fiction or Science: *The Calcutta Chromosome*	144
6. Beyond the Commonwealth: Amitav Ghosh and Indian Writing in English	164
Topics for Discussion	178
Bibliography	185

Series Editor's Preface

Contemporary Indian Writers In English (CIWE) presents critical commentaries on some of the best-known names in the genre. With the high visibility of Indian writing in English in academic, critical, pedagogic and readerly circles, there is a perceivable demand for lucid yet rigorous introductions to many of its authors and genres. Indian writing in English, in each of its genres — fiction, poetry, non-fiction and drama — has a diversity of themes, forms and styles. CIWE titles explore precisely this rich diversity. Attention to the narrative form of the novels/poems is accompanied by a detailed reading of the central themes in the author. The plan of the series is to provide as complete a survey of an author's oeuvre as possible, within a manageable length.

CIWE seeks to strike a balance between providing an introductory study as well as a critical appraisal of the writer's work. The former serves the informed, non-specialist reader, while the latter suits the academic – essay/seminar/assignment in literature classrooms. The theoretical approaches are wide-ranging – from structural analysis of narrative to feminist literary criticism. Every text in the series provides biographical information, close textual analysis, a survey of the author's chief thematic concerns, bibliographic information for those who wish to pursue further reading, and a comprehensive list of topics for discussion. The last section is meant to aid further reflection on the author or text, and is indicative of the potential every author in the Indian writing in English 'canon' possesses.

Amitav Ghosh is indisputably one of the most important novelists and essayists today. A novelist with an extraordinary sense of history and place, Ghosh locates an individual's drama in the general, often uncontrollable, sweep of humanity's destiny and actions. From the Partition to colonial science to colonialism, Ghosh is interested in the ways in which the violence of history, geography and politics alters lives. An extraordinarily fine stylist and narrator, Ghosh is also, quite often, a dense read.

John Hawley provides a lucid, friendly and thorough introduction to the fiction and essays of Ghosh. Hawley elaborates and critically examines Ghosh's concerns with communalism, colonial power, historiography while also providing an understanding of Ghosh's narrative modes and styles. This introduction will be useful for those who are interested in understanding the work of one of the most significant voices in Indian and world literature.

CIWE texts, it is hoped, will not only popularize the genre of Indian writing in English further, but also encourage serious critical work on it.

Pramod K. Nayar
Department of English
University of Hyderabad,
India.

1. The Writer, his Contexts and his Themes

> Like many Indians I grew up on stories of other countries: places my parents and relatives had lived in or visited before the birth of the Republic of India in 1947. (Afterword, *Burma: Something Went Wrong* (Photos by Chan Chao))

> Suddenly she understood why people arranged marriages for their children: it was a way of shaping the future to the past, of cementing one's ties to one's memories and to one's friends. . . how wonderful it might be, the bringing together of so many stories. (*The Glass Palace:* 199)

Amitav Ghosh's novels brim with interesting themes set against fascinating historical backdrops. These two quotes are a good place to begin our discussion of Amitav Ghosh, however, because they place a salutary emphasis on the third of the equation that might otherwise be short-changed: the stories. Ghosh's roots are in journalism and academic writing – investigation and analysis, a revelation of subterranean connections and patterns – but first and foremost, and overriding all the many *ideas* that inform his work are the stories, the Dickensian proliferation of characters whose lives engage us and who take us to some richly imagined places and times.

First, though, a consideration of the writer's personal history, his own "places" and "times". Amitav Ghosh was born in Calcutta on 11 July 1956. His father was first a Lieutenant Colonel in the army and, later, a diplomat. Ghosh grew up in East Pakistan, in Sri Lanka, Iran and India. He attended the Doon School in Dehra Dun, and then received a BA (with honours) in History from St. Stephen's College, Delhi University in 1976 and an MA in Sociology from the University in 1978. He received a diploma in Arabic from the Institut Bourguiba des Langues Vivantes, in Tunis, Tunisia, in 1979, and then a DPhil. (PhD) in Social Anthropology from (St. Edmund's Hall) Oxford University in 1982. As part of that course, in 1980 he went to Egypt to do field work in the village of Lataifa. He worked for a while as a journalist for *The Indian Express* newspaper in New Delhi. Since then he has been a Visiting Fellow at the Centre for Social Sciences, at Trivandrum, Kerala (1982-83), a Visiting Professor of Anthropology at the University of Virginia (1988), the University of Pennsylvania (1989), the American University in Cairo (1994), and Columbia University (1994-97), and Distinguished Professor of Comparative Literature at Queens College of the City University of New York (1999-2003). In the Spring of 2004, he was Visiting Professor in the department of English at Harvard University. He spends part of each year in Calcutta, but lives in New York with his wife, Deborah Baker, an editor at Little Brown and Company, and their children, Leela and Nayan.

In 1984, a momentous year for India; there was separatist violence in the Punjab, a military attack on the Sikh temple of Amritsar, the assassination of Prime Minister Indira Gandhi, there were riots following the assassination, and there was the gas disaster in Bhopal. It was as if George Orwell's infamous date for the apocalypse had been set with India in mind. Many peoples' lives were irrevocably shaken by these events and, it seems, Ghosh's was one of them. "Looking back," Ghosh writes, "I see that the experiences of that period were profoundly important to my development as a writer." ("The Ghosts of Mrs. Gandhi", *The Imam and the Indian*: 46)

> I was twenty-eight. The city I considered home was Calcutta, but New Delhi was where I had spent all my adult life except for a few years away in England and Egypt. I had returned to India two years before, upon completing a doctorate in Oxford, and recently found a teaching job at Delhi University. But it was in the privacy of my baking rooftop hutch that my real life was lived. I was writing my first novel, in the classic fashion, perched in a garret. (46-47)

Already he was identifying writing as his "real" life, distinct finally from his teaching and research. But the subjects he would choose to address and the style he would choose to employ were still in flux. The events of 1984 seem to have solidified his thinking in both regards.

The riots were directed principally against Sikh men, and as their ramifications unfolded "it was not just grief I felt," he writes. "Rather, it was a sense of something slipping loose, of a mooring coming untied somewhere within" (48). Over 2500 died in Delhi alone. "Like many other members of my generation," writes Ghosh,

> I grew up believing that mass-slaughter of the kind that accompanied the Partition of India and Pakistan, in 1947, could never happen again. But that morning, in the city of Delhi, the violence had reached the same level of intensity ... How do you explain to someone who has spent a lifetime cocooned in privilege that a potentially terminal rent has appeared in the wrapping? (52 – 53)

He had been writing *The Circle of Reason* in that "baking rooftop hutch," and its style was very much in a Salman Rushdie vein of imaginative serio-comic storytelling – a flight of fancy that had only the loosest ties to actual historical events. But 1984 changed all that: it is as though the next novel, *The Shadow Lines*, was written by someone else entirely. Here the style is, if anything, more sophisticated – but less fantastic. Here the history of Partition is very real, indeed, but its broad strokes are used to paint a backdrop against which a personal struggle of the young protagonist and his family gets the spotlight. Why this change happened (and continues) is one of the questions that we will want to explore as we move through his corpus of writing.

This was not to be the final shaping influence in his work, of course. Indeed, Ghosh has by now become a bit notorious in his bold embrace of new genres and styles when he undertakes a new project. In her review of *Dancing in Cambodia, At Large in Burma* for *India Star*, Meenakshi Mukherjee speaks for many when she observes:

> We have now come to expect each new Amitav Ghosh book to be different from what has appeared before. The wistful evocation of memory to reflect on divisions of land and people in *The Shadow Lines* (1988) had nothing in common with the disjointed magic realism of his apprentice novel, *The Circle of Reason* (1986). Neither, however, prepared any reader for the febrile frenzy of *The Calcutta Chromosome* (1996) where the history of malaria research is spliced with this story of subaltern subversions of Western science. The conflation of genres in [*Dancing in Cambodia*] is quite unlike what was tried by Ghosh's other non-fiction work, *In An Antique Land* (1992). In *Dancing in Cambodia*, travel, history, cultural commentary, political reportage shade into one another, the whole permeated with ruminations on freedom, power, violence and pain. Other histories and other geographies come alive and align with our own through Ghosh's translucent prose.

Mukherjee underscores in this review Amitav Ghosh's refusal to be categorised, his rebellion against the templates of genre. Are his books, such as *In An Antique Land* or *The Calcutta Chromosome*, any one genre?

In an interview with Sheela Reddy in 2002, Ghosh suggests that his future writing may go in still newer directions, at least in their themes if not their forms. "In some way," he told Reddy,

> the riots [of the '60s and '70s] didn't change anything... To me, that was the most disquieting aspect of that kind of social violence. But since Sept. 11, something has changed very drastically in the world. Perhaps it is a symptom rather than a cause. The whole system of nation-states is coming under increasing strain. The rich countries are essentially more and more a single unit: borders don't really apply. At the bottom of the scale, in countries like Pakistan and Burma, again borders have melted away and there's a general collapse of the state. I think we are at a point where the ideal of the nation as a way of organising society is no longer holding.

In this ominous description of our age, we see a first suggestion of Ghosh's recurring themes: the role of the individual in the broad sweep of political events; the dubious nature of borders, whether between nations and peoples or between one literary genre and another; the role of memory in one's recovery of identity in the march of time; the role of the artist in society; the importance of narrative in shaping history. We are about to see how these themes have played themselves out in his novels and essays, but it would be tantalising to imagine how they may develop in coming years. I conducted an interview with Ghosh in the summer of 2004, as he was about to leave on an author's tour to promote *The Hungry Tide*. Here is what was on his mind at that time:

JH: In a recent interview with Frederick Luis Aldama for *World Literature Today*, when asked about the various genres in which you write, you responded that you did not really consider them to be completely distinct from each other. You note that you studied History and Anthropology, and that you prefer narration because "in the end my real interest is in the predicament of individuals. And in this I don't think there is that much difference between fiction and non-fiction." Perhaps like most good novelists, you prefer the concrete and idiosyncratic over the abstract. Could you expand on this approach, please, and say a bit about how you imagine a character, how you choose their predicaments, how you insert them into their larger historical context.

AG: My fundamental interest is in people – in individuals and their specific predicaments. If history is of interest to me it is because it provides instances of unusual and extraordinary predicaments. For instance, take Arjun at the battle of Jitra (*The Glass Palace*): his life is brought to crisis by a historical circumstance. He shares this circumstance with many others, but he responds to it in a fashion that is particular to himself. This crisis is more dramatic than any I could have thought up on my own, and that is why it is so rewarding to look at history carefully. But to me the historical (or non-fictional) aspect of the situation is interesting only insofar as it creates a unique predicament for a character. In regard to anthropology I think it would be best if I quoted from an interview I did last year (I don't think this was ever published): "In some ways, my training as an anthropologist was of great help to me as a writer. I spent a year living in a small village in Egypt, and during this time I kept an exhaustive diary, in which I made extensive notes about my conversations with people, and the things I saw around me. Not only did this teach me to observe what I was seeing; it also taught me how to translate raw experience on to the page. It was in a way, the best kind of training a novelist could have and it has stood me in good stead over the years. Much of my writing has been influenced by this training. To this day I have a keen interest in observing the world around me, in listening to other people's stories, in trying to imagine and understand ways of looking at the world that differ from my own. At the same time, I also felt the limitations of anthropology very keenly. My essential interest is in people and their lives, histories and predicaments. There is not much room for this in formal anthropology, which is more interested in abstractions and generalisations. So I realised very early that I did not share the basic concerns of anthropology and that fiction was my proper métier."

JH: You mention that Marcel Proust, Gabriel Garcia Marquez and Ford Madox Ford have had a large influence in what you choose to emphasise in your own writing. How have they? Who are some others that have been influential? You also mention in the Aldama interview that "time interests [you] very much," and that you find it to be "the central element in narrative." This comes as no surprise to anyone who has read a few chapters of any of your novels. A few of the works are strictly sequential, but the vast majority of them typically carry on two or more stories in two or more periods of history, each ongoing in the present, and ultimately interlocking and affecting each other. It can throw the unsuspecting reader into confusion for a brief time, and then tends to draw him or her into a web of intriguing ramifications and questions of how one thing connects to another, how the choice of an individual in one decade or century may shape the future prospects of the next several generations. Does this come from your interest in History – or, at any rate, how did you decide to "wrap" one age in another like this? What philosophy of narrative technique, in other words, would you say you find to be most compatible to your purposes as a novelist?

AG: The narrative structure of Ford Madox Ford's *The Good Soldier* made a huge impression on me when I first read it, in my teens. My interest in Proust was born when I found out, many years later, that Madox Ford had been influenced by *Remembrance of Things Past*. However I did not read *Remembrance of Things Past* until 1985, after I'd written my first novel *The Circle of Reason*. This was about the time that I was starting my second novel, *The Shadow Lines* and Proust certainly had a great impact on the book. I think in retrospect that one of the reasons why Proust made such an impression was that his work seemed to me to represent an alternative modernism. Until then I had been exposed mainly to the Anglo-Irish-American variant of modernism, which is of course, deeply hostile to the narrative or representational impulse. Proust's work on the other hand, offered many very interesting possibilities so far as narrative is concerned. And from the start of my writing life my fundamental engagement has been with narrative (indeed this was one of the reasons why I wanted to write fiction).

In any event, Proust's influence on *The Shadow Lines* is clearly evident I think, even in the structure of its sentences. Similarly, it was in deference to Proust that the narrator of *The Shadow Lines* was left unnamed. But Proust's influence is evident also in the ways in which time and space are collapsed in the narrative of *The Shadow Lines*. I remember that at the time my ambition was to do with space what Proust had done with time: that is, to make completely different instances of a continuum immanent in each other.

JH: Borders – literal or metaphorical – continue to draw your attention in your various novels and essays: the arbitrary nature of national borders, the shifting characteristics of the boundaries separating one individual from another in personal relationships. Given your personal experience of the divisions between Pakistan and India, etc., perhaps this would be inevitable. Nonetheless, in your work it takes on a metaphysical and iconic significance. Could you reflect on why this is so?

AG: What interested me first about borders was their arbitrariness, their constructedness – the ways in which they are 'naturalised' by modern political myth-making. I think this interest arose because of some kind of inborn distrust of anything that appears to be 'given' or taken-for-granted. This is why I distrust also the lines that people draw between fiction and non-fiction. I think these lines are drawn in order to manipulate our ways of thought: that is why they must be disregarded.

JH: In the Aldama interview you take issue with those like Fredric Jameson and Homi Bhabha who characterise "Third World" novels as being essentially about nation and nation building. In your view, "the nation is not, as it were, the central imaginative unit," and you set about demonstrating this by telling stories in which families "actually span nations." Families, in effect, become the central imaginative unit in most of your novels, and you suggest that "you make your family your nation." *The Calcutta Chromosome*, perhaps, is an exception, but nation certainly plays no role in that work, either. One might even say that there is a new and broader definition of family even in that work of science fiction. Does the novelist have a role to play in the "nation building" to which these theorists refer? Is there a related role for the novelist as prophet, as the speaker of truth to power, as, in Shelley's phrase, an "unacknowledged legislator of the world"? More broadly, what is the role of an artist in today's society?

AG: In fact, it is precisely the First World novel that is most commonly about nations and nation building. Consider for instance, the peculiar obsession with 'Englishness' that runs through so much of nineteenth and twentieth - century British writing. This is even more strikingly evident in the US today, where nothing seems to be of interest unless it is American ('the *American* family') or has 'America' or 'American' in its title (witness such phenomena as *American Beauty, Riding in Cars in America* etc.). In countries like India the nation as such is still too young and too tenuous an institution to have acquired this axiomatic status. So far as the artist's role in society is concerned, it's certainly true that in India writers are subject to pressures that seem not to exist in the US. I was in the US during the first Gulf War and I was very struck by how no major American writer seemed to have an opinion about it. This would be inconceivable in India, where the lives of writers and artists are highly politicised. But as I see it, it is precisely because the pressures are so great that Indian artists have to be very careful in limiting their role in politics – that is why we have to pick and choose our involvements. Otherwise it is very easy to be swamped by the pressures – and indeed this has happened to several Indian artists. Personally speaking, I never allow myself to forget that my most important public commitment is to my work: if this was not so I would not be a writer; I would be a politician. But a writer is also a citizen, not just of a country but of the world. When I feel strongly about some issue I think it's my duty to express my views as cogently and forcefully as possible. This was why I undertook to write *Countdown* in 1998, after the nuclear tests of that year. I was then deep into *The Glass Palace* and absolutely the last thing I wanted was to interrupt myself. But I felt that this was an issue that left me no choice. But I don't think that it's possible to legislate for everyone on this matter. Artists are nothing if not individualistic and each must, and ought to, forge their role according to their own ideas and desires.

JH: Related to the previous question, you mention to Aldama that in writing *The Glass Palace* you "felt that [you'd] been entrusted with the story, a story that was beyond [you] and greater than [you]." One notices throughout your work an abiding concern for what Gayatri Spivak and others have discussed as the voice of the "subaltern." More simply put, you are apparently concerned with those who do not have a voice in society, who are overlooked by history, who get swallowed up by the powerful, and by time. Where does this interest find its roots? What are you hoping to accomplish?

AG: I am sure at some level I have been deeply influenced by the ideas of the 'subaltern studies' group. The founder of *Subaltern Studies*, Ranajit Guha, is a close friend and so are many other members of the group. As you may know I have even published in *Subaltern Studies*. More generally speaking however, I think I share some of the concerns of the *Subaltern Studies* group because I am from the same milieu as many of the group's members. But it is true also that anyone who looks into Indian history must necessarily be amazed by how little is actually known about it. And I don't just mean the history of 'subaltern' groups, but even of dissenting elites (for example the story of the founders of the Indian National Army is unknown to most Indians). As for the history of the Indian presence in Burma, it is completely unknown – there is very little written about it. In this sense I felt I was bearing a double burden when I was writing *The Glass Palace*. When an American writes a historical novel he or she can generally rely on the historians to have done the research. I didn't have this luxury available to me. I had to do much of the primary research while also telling a story.

JH: What have you thought of the reviews of your work? *The Shadow Lines*, for example, is pretty canonical now in India, but not necessarily so elsewhere – though widely praised. Are there any interpretations that have struck you as strikingly wrong? What in your view is the reception in the West, in general, of writers from India or Africa or, to find a portmanteau, from the Third World? And what of this notion of the cosmopolitan writer who travels about and lives in this large city and then that one – does such a writer still speak for any particular culture, or has he or she gradually become – for lack of a more graceful term – a location of globalisation?

AG: For the last many years I have generally avoided reading reviews, theses and critical articles about my work. There's often a temptation to enter into a dialogue with your critics and as I see it, there can be nothing productive in this for a novelist. The only reviews I actually seek out and read nowadays are those written in Bengali. I can't account for why this is so, but it just is. But I do think the quality of reviewing in America is extraordinarily good, far better than in the UK or in Europe. I know for sure that some of the most perceptive reviews of my early books were written in the US. You ask about the reception of 'Third World Writers' in the West. This has changed dramatically over the last fifteen to twenty years. It is no longer possible for critics to sneer at our books or to dismiss them out of hand. I think this is due in large part to critics such as Edward Said, Homi Bhabha and Gayatri Spivak. Between them they have succeeded in shifting the critical ground in literary studies.

JH: Do you have a favourite among your novels?

AG: No.

JH: In *The Circle of Reason*, *The Hungry Tide* and *The Calcutta Chromosome*, and here and there in various of your other novels, you demonstrate an interest in science. In the first two, it also seems tied in with questions of obsession, and in the last, with questions of metaphysics or even specifically Hindu philosophy and definition of individual identity. Could you expand on the role you see science playing in your work, and in the contemporary world. Related to this, you seem interested in science as a "way of knowing" or a kind of matrix for one's imagination of the world – as a mechanism for setting a particular set of questions for oneself, as opposed to the questions that others might set for themselves (e.g., a historian, as opposed to a medical researcher seeking the vector for malaria). You mention that in researching various of your books you got heavily immersed in new worlds – the Sundarbans, for example, or the mercantile world of the Indian Ocean some centuries ago. What is the role of knowledge and imagination in your work?

AG: I am deeply interested in the methods of knowledge and in our ways of knowing. This is, as you rightly point out, one of the central themes in my work.

JH: Do you think you may still plumb your childhood schooling for a novel?

AG: Maybe, but I doubt it.

JH: You have lived in New York for some time now. Will the events of 9/11 play a role in your future work? Do you have any views of how the destruction of the World Trade Center has changed the United States and, perhaps, the world? Or was it rather a dramatic unveiling of something that was always there?

In response to this final question, Ghosh referred me to his 16 December 2001 interview with Rahul Sagar for *The Hindu*.

AG: I believe that much has gone wrong with the American relationship with the world, political and economic, over the last decade. But if you ask me whether there is a direct connection between this and the World Trade Center attacks, my answer is no, I do not think there is... I believe that what is happening in Palestine is horrific and the US should certainly reconsider its policies there. But does this mean that there is a direct link between the sufferings of the Palestinians and the World Trade Center attacks?

If you ask me whether Palestine was the fundamental motivating factor behind the World Trade Center attacks I would say that the evidence is to the contrary.

Or, take the suggestion that the World Trade Center attacks were in some sense caused by globalisation. The people who have suffered most from globalisation are sub-Saharan Africans - but these are not the people who are turning to terror. Most of the terrorists were from the oil-rich countries of the Arabian peninsula; globalisation had given them lives where everything was taken care of and they never had to do any work. If they were concerned about oppression, the first people they would have tried to liberate would be the huge servant class of foreigners that keeps their countries going - the millions of South and South-East Asians who live there without any political rights whatsoever. None of them have ever uttered a word on that score. The fact is that globalisation's most effective opponents are the thousands of young people who have become active in the anti-globalisation movement. Many of these activists are Westerners and many are American. So if the terrorists attacked Americans because of globalisation, then in fact they were also attacking the people who were their potential allies in that struggle.

I think we must be careful even in making the assumption that an articulate grievance existed at all. I have heard it said that the very enormity of the World Trade Center attack and the multiple suicides involved indicate the existence of a monumental grievance. But in some parts of India even such events as the death of an important public figure sometimes lead to dozens of grisly suicides. What is the grievance here, except mortality itself?

(Excerpt from the interview in *The Hindu*)

The implications of much of the foregoing will be discussed at greater length in the next chapter, in which Ghosh's essays come into play. But before we move on, we would do well to underscore two of the most interesting themes that recur in much of what follows.

The first is the novelist's abiding interest in listening to the voice of the anonymous individual, the typical person who is unrecorded in "history" – an obscure slave and his master in *In An Antique Land*, a mysterious urchin living in an Indian train station in *The Calcutta Chromosome*, an overlooked fisherman in *The Hungry Tide*. John Thieme is among the many who have observed that Ghosh, in all his writings, achieves a large degree of imaginative empathy, "the product of a humanist concern to transcend culturally constructed differences. . . . [H]is concern with the recuperation and rendering of individual experiences operates against the kind of totalising theory that habitually consigns subalternity to oblivion" (Internet). Another very perceptive critic, one with a background in psychology, writes that

> [Ghosh] is interested in what might in Cultural Studies terms, but also in Literary Studies terms, be called the articulation of the fragile subject in everyday life. . . . the subject who is fragile because ordinary, and interesting because it is precisely the ordinary that slips through the fingers of the academic historian or even the methodologically scrupulous social anthropologist. (Samir Dayal: 105)

The other theme that we must mention, and that underpins so many of the others, is one that is designated by that catch-all term, postcoloniality. Ghosh seeks to approach the topic from a new perspective that does not privilege the coloniser by accepting the manichean definition of West and East. Instead, as John Skinner writes, Ghosh's concern is "not only with coloniser and colonised, but with both historical and contemporary relations between different colonised groups. Not so much 'the empire writes back,' then, as 'the empire writes home'" (Skinner). For Ghosh this conversation among equals (equals with a history of exploitation by the West) implies an underscoring of the *duties* that are now placed at their doorstep. As he told Rahul Sagar in a December 2001 interview for *The Hindu*:

> For me the most important lessons of the anti-colonial struggle are those that emphasise responsibility. . . . I think we Indians owe a great deal of gratitude to our leaders of the early twentieth century, for their emphasis was as much on building a society as it was on expelling the colonialist.

In short, Ghosh does not skirt difficult questions and he does not offer soothing answers that are sure to please his readers. His work is serious stuff. But it is also full of fun, as is any good story.

2. A Writer Situated in a History and in a Place

Ghosh's Non-Fiction

Dancing in Cambodia, At Large in Burma (1998), *Countdown* (1999), Ghosh's afterword to Chan Chao's book of photography, *Burma: Something Went Wrong* (2000), and *The Imam and the Indian: Prose Pieces* (2002)

This chapter considers Amitav Ghosh's non-fictional writing. Viewed together, the collected essays demonstrate his chief concerns:

- The nuclearisation of the subcontinent (*Countdown*; *The Ghat of the Only World*)

- The current political crisis in Burma and Cambodia (*Dancing in Cambodia, At Large in Burma*; *The Global Reservation*; *Burma: Something Went Wrong*)

- The maintenance of cultural heritage (*Dancing in Cambodia*; *The Hunger of Stones*; *The Human Comedy in Cairo*)

- Pre-European commerce between India and Africa (*The Slave of MS. H.6*)

- Fundamentalism (*The Imam and the Indian*; *An Egyptian in Baghdad*; *The Fundamentalist Challenge*)

- Anthropology and Economics in local communities (*Categories of Labour and the Orientation of the Fellah Economy*; *The Relations of Envy in an Egyptian Village*)

- The Diaspora (*The Imam and the Indian*; *Tibetan Dinner*; *The Diaspora in Indian Culture*; *The March of the Novel Through History*)

Viewed with a less narrow focus, many of these pieces share in common the author's abiding concern for the impact of broad historical movements on individuals caught up in events beyond their control, the importance of connections between the past and the present, and the desirability of finding avenues for communication that obviate nationalistic manias.

It is unusual for a novelist to produce as rich a body of essays as Amitav Ghosh has. He did work as a journalist, of course, and perhaps has always had an interest in reaching different audiences – some prefer reading fiction, others prefer shorter essays on less obviously "imagined" topics. Yet even in these more prosaic works Ghosh typically tells one story after another, eliciting from readers a sense of engagement that might otherwise be missing. We can begin our discussion of Ghosh by looking at these essays in one extended sweep, since they are usually looked at only in passing, as a support for discussions of his fiction. If we see what issues motivate his political, historical, and anthropological work, though, we will be well-positioned to consider the informing interests that manifest themselves in other ways throughout his novels.

Dancing in Cambodia, At Large in Burma

This small book is a collection of three essays previously published in journals: "Dancing in Cambodia," from *Granta* 44 (Summer of 1993), "Stories in Stones," from *The Observer Magazine*, 16 January, 1994, and "At Large in Burma," previously published in *The New Yorker* on 12 August, 1996. The first essay contains several illustrations by the French artist Auguste Rodin from his encounter with the dancers who are the subject of Ghosh's essay. It typifies the writer's tendency to illustrate bold historical themes through simple individual (and often serendipitous) meetings.

In fact, "Dancing in Cambodia" interweaves *two* historical encounters. The first is the visit to Marseilles in June of 1906 of King Sisowath of Cambodia and a troupe of nearly a hundred classical dancers and musicians from the royal palace at Phnom Penh. The second is Amitav Ghosh's visit to Cambodia in January of 1993 in search of Pol Pot's sister-in-law, who was said to be one of the country's greatest dancers – in fact, a national treasure.

Contemporary newspaper accounts suggest that the French were entranced by the exotic King and even more so by the dancers. Their emotional and curious response is perhaps a classic example of orientalisation: "For weeks now," writes Ghosh,

> the Marseilles newspapers had been full of tantalising snippets of information: it was said that the dancers entered the palace as children and spent their lives in seclusion ever afterwards; that their lives revolved entirely around the royal family; that several were the King's mistresses and had even borne him children; that some of them had

A Writer Situated in a History and in a Place

never stepped out of the palace grounds until this trip to France. (3)

In fact, whereas "they had expected perhaps a troop of heavily-veiled, voluptuous Salomés, they were not quite prepared for the lithe, athletic women they encountered. ... nor indeed, was the rest of Europe" (4). Interestingly, so indescribable did they appear, so far outside the expected boundaries of categorisation, that one observer later wrote that "they seem to belong to no definite sex" (4). The visit to France by the troupe was Cambodia's contribution to the "Exposition Coloniale," which celebrated France's colonial possessions. They were simply one of the many wonders that fascinated the French who took the occasion to reflect on their global empire. As Ghosh notes, "there was little by way of exotic and opulent fantasy that the exhibition did not offer, from Tunisian palaces to timber-studded West African mosques and Indo-Chinese pavilions " (2).

Ghosh goes on, however, to describe King Sisowath as a neo-colonial collaborator who sought to imitate the French, whereas the brother whom he succeeded to the throne, Norodom, had been for forty years an annoyance to the French. Sisowath's intermediary with the French was his interpreter, minister Thiounn. His grandson, Thiounn Mumm, later became immensely influential among the Cambodian elite who studied in France. Ghosh sees his complex intermediary role as "immediately recognisable to anyone who has ever inhabited the turbulent limbo of the Asian or African student in Europe – that curious circumstance of social dislocation and emotional turmoil that for more than a century now has provided the site for some of the globe's most explosive political encounters" (24). Note how Ghosh sets the stage, peoples it with fascinating characters, and then rather broadly interprets the play as paradigmatic of many similar events throughout history. Among those who came under Thiounn Mumm's sway was one Saloth Sar. In 1952, Thiounn Mumm apparently inducted Saloth Sar into the French Communist party, with hideous future consequences.

As Ghosh recounts his tale of past events, he returns us to the time in which he personally enters the historical chain of events. He hopes to speak with Chea Samy because she is old enough to have known King Sisowath – and, more importantly, Princess Soumphady. Princess Soumphady had been in charge of the dancers, and in fact had been a surrogate mother for them; thus, Chea Samy would be a direct connection to the country's terpsichorean tradition. A woman named Molyka is Ghosh's friend, and it is she who will escort him to Chea Samy. Molyka is a thirty-one-year-old mid-level civil servant who had braved a great deal in her own life: in 1975, when she was thirteen, the Khmer Rouge had taken Phnom Penh and she and her extended family of fourteen people were evacuated to a labour camp in the province of Kompong Thom. Three years later, ten of these were dead, including her father, two brothers, and a sister. Her mother was now a terrified woman; her brother was guilt-ridden for having accidentally betrayed their father. Understandably, Molyka was quite hesitant to meet Chea Samy, since the dancer, after all, was Pol Pot's sister-in-law.

When Chea Samy was a child, dance was one of the few means by which a commoner could gain entry into the palace. She was taken there in 1925 when she was six. When King Sisowath died two years later, his son's favourite mistress, Luk Khun Meak, who was a dancer, brought to the palace several of her own villagers, including Chea

Samy's future husband and his brother, known as Saloth Sar. He was later to be known only as Pol Pot. Because of these palace connections, Saloth Sar was given a scholarship to study electronics in Paris in 1949. While there, he was heavily influenced by several well-known leftists and communists, and upon his return three years later to Cambodia, he began working for the Indochina Communist Party. In 1963, he disappeared, and "emerged" in 1975 as Pol Pot, when the Khmer Rouge seized power. Again, notice how Ghosh weaves individual lives, often of characters whom traditional history has overlooked, into an intricate tapestry of connections.

In 1979, the Vietnamese brought about the collapse of Pol Pot's regime, and the many evacuees began straggling back to their villages. During the intense period of his reign, however, as many as 90 per cent of the country's pre-revolution artists were killed. As Ghosh puts it: "It was a war on history itself, an experiment in the re-invention of society. No regime in history had ever before made so systematic and sustained an attack on the middle class. Yet, if the experiment was proof of anything at all, it was ultimately of the indestructibility of the middle class, of its extraordinary tenacity and resilience; its capacity to preserve its forms of knowledge and expression through the most extreme kinds of adversity" (10). Why does he draw this conclusion? Since many of the survivors had had to invent imaginary histories for themselves during the Pol Pot years (in order to avoid extermination), the time afterwards was one of personal struggle to remember who, in fact, they were. At the same time, it was a period of reconstruction of the artistry and culture of the nation. In Ghosh's words, "they had to start from the beginning, literally, like ragpickers, piecing their families, their roofs, their lives together from the little that was left" (18). In reinventing Cambodia's culture, "they began to create the means of denying Pol Pot his victory" (18).

Ghosh blames the French for a good bit of Pol Pot's extremes, starting with the racism the madman may have picked up from them. In any case, Ghosh describes the Khmer Rouge agenda as racist nationalism aimed at Cambodia's Vietnamese minority. He quotes the dictator's brother as believing that the troubles began when Saloth Sar (soon to become "Pol Pot") went off to Paris. The author then makes an interesting comparison – between Pol Pot and King Sisowath – and broadens his observation still further. "The trip to France," he writes,

> 'the dream of his whole life,' evidently cast King Sisowath's mind into the same kind of turmoil, the same tumult of shock and bewilderment that has provoked generations of displaced students – the Gandhi's, the Senghor's, and the Kenyatta's, amongst thousands of their less illustrious countrymen – to close their doors upon the cold unfamiliarity of wintry Western cities and lock themselves into their rooms to pour their hearts out in letters, recording their impressions for those they had left at home. (39)

The émigrés he mentions are strikingly different from Saloth Sar, are they not? In fact, Pol Pot may have locked himself away in his Parisian garret and spent a lot of his time thinking and writing, but he shared very few of his thoughts with his family. His mind turned inward, towards a fundamentalist apocalyptic vision of social change. He admired the French Revolution's Robespierre, and Ghosh quotes the playwright who had that madman announce that "Terror is an emanation of virtue" (50).

King Sisowath chose the opposite path toward social transformation: rather than burning his culture to the ground, he offered an exhortation to his countrymen to imitate French technology. The King's choice seems to have been the one that is now more influential in former colonies, but Ghosh, while clearly repulsed by Pol Pot, nonetheless concludes that "no one is likely to thank" Sisowath for his accommodating attitude toward the coloniser (42).

Happily, Ghosh ends his essay on an upbeat note, recording that the dance tradition that King Sisowath had brought to Marseilles and that Pol Pot had nearly succeeded in obliterating, was restored to its former glory in 1988. Chea Samy and a few others like her had managed to pass along what they knew, and in that year, classical Cambodian dance was once again performed in Phnom Penh. Thus, the storyteller shows his knack for leading us back in time, through various overgrown footpaths, demonstrating interesting forgotten incidents that oddly intersect, and then bringing us comfortably back to the spot where we began.

The second essay in the book, "Stories in Stone," is prompted by Ghosh's visit to Angkor Wat, the twelfth-century Cambodian temple. He provocatively describes this building, the largest single religious edifice in the world, as "a monument to the power of the story" (54) – principally because it is encrusted with religious iconography, and also because its own history as a building is heavily overlain with the biographies of kings and other potentates. Ghosh is also fascinated by the paradoxical use to which the image of the building is put: the West sees it as stereotypical of the romance of lost civilisations, "of lost glory, devoured by time" (56), whereas in Cambodia itself it seems to represent *modernity*, of all things. At least, its image is reproduced on representations of such unlikely products as beer, flags, airlines, military uniforms, banks, etc. Most striking to the author is the fact that the building is still used for religious purposes, though this less "modern" activity is tucked inconspicuously into a corner of the central courtyard and has been there, functioning in that capacity, for centuries. What was "discovered" by the French explorer Henri Mouhot in the nineteenth century was not this ongoing *religious* structure, but

> a mirror . . .of the Imperial State. . . . For an entire generation of Cambodians . . ., it became the opposite of itself: an icon that represented a break with the past – a token of the country's belonging, not within the medieval, but rather the contemporary world. (60)

The third essay in the book, "At Large in Burma" is a reflection on the author's three meetings with Aung San Suu Kyi. In fact, the first encounter was more than a meeting: in 1980, Ghosh and Aung San Suu Kyi were students at Oxford, and Ghosh remembers her as being a 35-year-old "leading a life of quiet, exiled domesticity on a leafy street in North Oxford, bringing up two sons, then aged seven and three, and writing occasional articles for scholarly journals" (75). He was surprised, therefore, to see her photograph in a magazine eight years later, speaking into a microphone in Rangoon. His second and third meetings with her were in late 1995, when he attended two of her weekend public meetings that she conducted from her gateside. These were first conducted during the house arrest that had been imposed in 1989 and then lifted in July of 1995. She had been awarded the Nobel Prize for Peace, *in absentia*, in 1991. During his meeting with her in December of 1995, he had been struck by her public manner, which had none of the solemnity of demeanour that he had expected. In fact, she laughed a great deal. Ghosh's third meeting with her, however, in July of 1996, suggested that something had changed. He found her animated, but no longer light-hearted. She seemed more guarded in her response to his questions, as if anticipating a future role outside her house, in the world of politics.

Her involvement in the politics of her troubled country had been somewhat serendipitous, despite her lineage. Her mother had been Burma's ambassador to India for some years; her father, General Aung San, had led the Anti-Fascist People's Freedom League to a great victory in the 1947 election — but had been assassinated before he could take office. She, though, had only been two years old at the time. She had returned to Rangoon in 1988 principally because her mother had suffered a stroke there. Events overtook her during the visit, and she seemed tailor-made to stand as a connection to the last legitimate election in the country before the military had taken draconian control. In passing, one might notice once again Ghosh's interest in tracing connections through history. After several riots against SLORC ("the State Law and Order Restoration Council") she stepped forward for election, and was quickly put under house arrest.

Reflecting on the way that history can call unsuspecting people into roles of prominence, Ghosh uses the occasion of his visits to reflect on Burma's recent unfortunate history. He begins with General Ne Win's assumption of power in 1962, which closed the country to the outside world for three decades. During this time, it slipped into inaccessibility and its people lost touch with the passage of time. Burma had been the most developed country in the region, but fifty years later, on the eve of Ghosh's visit to the country, it had become one of the United Nations's ten *least* developed nations on earth. In the view of many, this tragic downward spiral was brought about by the civil strife that was waiting to erupt after the British pulled out (it had been British policy to favour minority groups over the ethnic Burmese). Many felt that General Aung San, who had negotiated the Panglong Agreement that offered a quasi-federal union to minority groups, was the only public figure who could avert a war. Upon his assassination and the imposition of military rule, therefore, the country began tearing itself apart.

While in Burma Ghosh also decides to visit the Karenni, one of the small groups who had been seeking some form of independence all this time, and who had been chased into ever-diminishing nomadic lives by the military. "There are," he writes, "five major Karenni refugee camps and together they form a minuscule, tight-knit nation-on-the-move, consisting of some six thousand people" (95). He asks himself this question: "What does it take . . . to sustain an insurgency for fifty years, to go on fighting a war that the rest of the world has almost forgotten?" (93). It is the sort of question that many ask these days, when some groups in unlikely places resist apparently overwhelming forces. Why *do* they do it?

It must be said that Ghosh does not offer a fully satisfying answer to the query, but he suggests that many of those involved in the conflict have by now forgotten the source of their grievance; they have simply accepted their current lives as the definition of themselves as a people. Others remember promises made to them (in this case, by the British) that subsequent Burmese governments refused to honour. But, perhaps surprisingly, Ghosh draws a rather pragmatic overall conclusion in the matter, a conclusion that has implications in conflicts elsewhere and, indeed, in several of the author's novels: "Burma's borders are undeniably arbitrary," he writes,

> ...the product of a capricious colonial history. But colonial officials cannot reasonably be blamed for the arbitrariness of the lines they drew. All boundaries are artificial: there is no such thing as a 'natural' nation, which has journeyed through history with its boundaries and ethnic composition intact. In a region as heterogeneous as South-East Asia, any boundary is sure to be arbitrary. On balance, Burma's best hopes for peace lie in maintaining intact the larger and more inclusive entity that history, albeit absent-mindedly, bequeathed to its population almost half a century ago. (100)

Some may be disappointed by such an apparently conservative reading of insurgency; others will respond favourably to its simple honesty.

Meanwhile, in his reflections on Aung San Suu Kyi, Ghosh comes face to face with her *ordinariness* as a human being. She is not super-human in any sense, and that is where her challenge lies. He notes that he is like many of the tourists and those from the foreign press who attend her gateside meetings:

> They were people like me, members of the world's vast, newspaper-reading middle class, people who took it for granted that there are no heroes among us. But Suu Kyi had proved us wrong. She lived the same kind of life, attended the same classes, read the same books and magazines, got into the same arguments. And she had shown us that the apparently soft and yielding world of books and words could sometimes forge a very fine kind of steel. (81-82)

There is nothing conservative in *that* conclusion.

Typically, Ghosh recognises that the "subaltern" in the world and in history, is inevitably ignored – unless someone like Suu Kyi comes along.

> In the post-modern world, politics is everywhere a matter of symbols, and the truth is that Suu Kyi is her own greatest political asset. It is only because Burma's 1988 democracy movement had a symbol, personified in Suu Kyi, that the world remembers it and continues to exert pressure on the current regime. (83)

Taken together, the three essays in this little book can be seen as the reporter's notebook, the anthropologist's series of observations, the historian's musings, that issue forth as *The Glass Palace* three years later. In that novel, the obvious political commitment of the essays is replaced by a richly imagined immersion in several generations of Indians and Burmese who live out their lives against the backdrop of history. As with so much of Ghosh's writing, these two books demonstrate his mind dividing itself into two types of analysis and narration.

Countdown

In a 17 July 2000 interview with *Outlook*, Ghosh was asked whether or not a sense of political engagement accompanies his sense of history. His response is intriguing, since he claims that he rarely reads newspapers and considers himself to be divorced from politics. But with the Pokharan blasts he felt called upon to speak up as a human being:

> A lot of the people I had to meet in order to write *Countdown* were horrible, as was the subject itself . . .

but I grit my teeth. I wish I hadn't had to do it, but I had to. It was a personal duty: any writer worth his salt has to tackle morality, particularly the morality of history.

This brief book, therefore, is a protest against the 1998 test of five nuclear devices at Pokharan by the Indian government, and a consideration of the current relations between India and Pakistan – a protest entered into less for political reasons and more from a sense of the *immorality* of the tests. The book is a part of Ghosh's larger project to imagine a "moral" history: not a history of morality, but a moral way of *imagining* history. The tests were carried out on 11 May 1998, two months after Atal Bihari Vajpayee and the Bharatiya Janata Party (B.J.P.) had come to power. Whatever exhilaration may have been felt by some in India quickly faded, when Pakistan tested nuclear devices of its own on 28 May. Ghosh reports that the rupee fell to a historic low, the stock market index plummeted, and prices soared.

Ghosh visits Pokharan and speaks with Manohar Joshi, a thirty-six-year-old man who had grown up in Pokharan and had been twelve in 1974, when Indira Gandhi's government had first tested a nuclear device in the region. Since that time many of his friends had contracted cancer and other physical problems. Near Pokharan is the old palace of Bikaner. While touring it and musing upon past glories, Ghosh recognises that "this was what the nuclearists wanted: to sign treaties, to be pictured with the world's powerful, to hang portraits on their walls, to become ancestors. On the bomb they had pinned their hopes of bringing it all back""(13). Such grand schemes of raising the nation's international profile came from K. Subrahmanyam, who was among those in India who looked at how the Soviet Union and the United States had avoided using their weapons and who had concluded that they were purely symbols. But Ghosh describes Subrahmanyam's followers as a new sect: "the bomb-cult," he writes, "represents the uprising of those who find themselves being pushed back from this table [of national and international power]: it is the rebellion of the rebelled-against, the insurrection of an elite" (18).

Ghosh meets up with George Fernandes at the Defence Ministry in New Delhi. Fernandes had apparently, at one time, thought of becoming a Catholic priest but had grown disillusioned with the human foibles of those in charge of the seminary. So he became a socialist. Ghosh describes him as having been the country's most prominent campaigner against human rights violations by the army. He later surprisingly helped the BJP come to power, despite their opposition to the secularism enshrined in India's constitution. Fernandes was the one who had approved the tests of 11 May. This fact, coupled with Ghosh's meeting with several other former idealists, forced him to ask the question: "How had matters come to such a pass that reasonable people could argue that the country needed to risk annihilation in order to repair the damage sustained by its self-esteem?" (30). The question has been asked by many in India and elsewhere who know that weapons that are invented are typically, in the course of nations, used.

Fernandes was taking a party of journalists with him to visit military installations in Kashmir, and Ghosh accompanies them. The author learns that the *generals* did not see the nuclear weapons simply as symbols, even if the politicians apparently did. They fly to Leh; at 12,000 feet in altitude it is the principal town in India's northernmost district. Ghosh is fascinated by the Line of

Control, by the talk of "cartographic aggression" (37) and the *notional* lines on maps that transformed the Siachen glacier into a battleground. A blunt Major tells him: "most of us here are from north India. We have more in common with the Pakistanis, if you don't mind my saying so, than we do with South Indians or Bengalis" (42). Later, Fernandes sounds near despair, doubting that either side wants to resolve the crisis, and describing both sides as *bleeding*. Ghosh writes:

> I came to be haunted by this metaphor, because of its undeniable appositeness – its evocation of the vendettas of peasant life along with its reference to the haemorrhaging of lives and resources on the glacier: how better to describe this conflict than through an image of two desperately poor protagonists, balancing upon a barren mountaintop, each with a pickaxe stuck in the other's neck, each propping the other up while waiting for him to bleed to death? (44)

In Fernandes' view, the crisis was due to the colonial mentality that India still embraced, and the replacement of true political parties with the rise of "castes and groups gathered around individuals . . . powerful sectional and regional interests [that] have prevented the formation of stable governments over the last few years" (46). Ghosh recognises that he is dealing with an intelligent man, but he wonders how he can cooperate in such a venture.

Soon after this, the author goes to Lahore, on what is his first visit to Pakistan. He finds the people there to be remarkably welcoming. But he found everyone he talked to *there*, at any rate, agreed that nuclear weapons were far more than symbols. As Qazi Hussain Ahmed, the leader of the Jam-aat-e-Islami, the principal religious party in Pakistan, tells Ghosh, "When a nation feels that it is likely to be defeated it can do anything to spare itself the shame" (55). Ghosh meets with Asma Jahangir, Pakistan's leading human rights lawyer, and is greatly impressed. "So far as I am concerned," he writes, "Asma Jahangir ranks with Burma's Aung San Suu Kyi as a figure of moral authority and an embodiment of courage" (58). She was most distressed by the influence of the Taliban in Pakistan and she speaks in stark and graphic terms of her confrontations with them in the courts. "I think," she tells him, "anyone who proposes orthodox Islam in Pakistan is actually strengthening the hands of the [BJP]. . . in the sense that fanaticism here brings fanaticism in India" (69). Both she and Qazi Hussain Ahmed, though opposed on some issues, indicted the ruling classes in Pakistan as looking out for their own interests rather than those of the nation. She also makes an interesting observation of national self-conceptions: "India wants to push a perception of South Asian identity," she tells Ghosh. "Pakistan [on the other hand] wants a South Asian identity and yet does not want it. It wants to leave the door open to an identity as a Middle Eastern country" (77).

Ghosh's stay in Pakistan ends with a visit to the Wagah border post, which is the only official crossing-point between India and Pakistan. There he observes the ritual that takes place every day at sunset when the flags of the two nations are lowered. He describes it as "a series of complicated drill manoeuvres, strutting and preening and stamping their feet like anxious roosters . . . sublimely comic" (85), a "precisely performed staging of a parodic enmity, produced by unseen regimes. . . as though we were in one of those cartoon-film situations where a train filled with looney-tune characters is heading towards a precipice – a chasm that is clearly visible to the audience and concealed only from the protagonists" (87-88). But when a film star shows up, "the border was instantly forgotten: the world of the screen became a reminder of real life" (87). A bit of Bollywood on the border, a hint of celluloid heroism overtakes the soldiers' sense of "reality." Ghosh seems to be fixated on this question of perception: Indian politicians preoccupied with a nostalgic return to historic empires through an entrance into the Atomic Club, as if it were a country club where the price of admission was well worth paying if it offered such unquestioned prestige.

Starkly countering such self-deception, Ghosh concludes his book with several pages of graphic description of what sort of destruction would be felt in New Delhi should a nuclear attack take place: "Almost everything that would be needed for the reconstruction of a settled society would perish within an instant of the blast," he notes (99). He suggests that his judgement of the rulers of India is similar to the judgement that Asma Jahangir and Qazi Hussain Ahmed had made of Pakistan's, namely, that "the pursuit of nuclear weapons in the subcontinent is the moral equivalent of civil war: the targets the rulers have in mind for these weapons are, in the end, none other than their own people" (106).

Burma: Something Went Wrong

This brief essay serves as the "Afterword" to a beautiful book of photographic portraits of eighty-eight individuals in Burma. Remarkably, not a single one is smiling. "Chan Chao's portraits," writes Ghosh,

> are remarkable for the honesty with which they portray the plight of the people who are trapped in this terrible

conflict. In his pictures, one sees despair, defeat, suffering and incomprehension; one sees also the courage, fatalism and hope that has sustained this war for more than half a century. As a record of human suffering, Chan Chao's portraits are as valuable as Roger Fenton's pictures of the Crimean War, Robert Capa's photographs of World War II and Sunil Janah's images of the Bengal famine of 1942. (126)

The photos make a nice figurative set of illustrations for his *Dancing in Cambodia* volume, and are published one year before *The Glass Palace*, in which a central character is a photographer who is as subversive as Aung San Suu Kyi.

The Imam and the Indian: Prose Pieces

This is a collection of eighteen prose pieces of various lengths and on a wide variety of subjects, previously published in journals. The earliest was written in 1985, and the most recent was published in 2002. Ghosh suggests that "the first five narratives... were all written in short and intensely focused periods of concentration" (vii). Thus, the piece that gives this collection its overall title, "The Imam and the Indian," was published in *Granta* in 1986. "I did not know it then, but the writing of this [piece] signalled the gestation of another project – my third book, *In An Antique Land* – which I was not to embark on until 1989" (vii). "Tibetan Dinner" came out in 1988, also in *Granta*. As he sits in a posh restaurant in Manhattan at a dinner organised by someone described very much like Richard Gere to raise money for the Tibetan cause, he recalls going to a ramshackle Tibetan restaurant in Delhi as a student.

> As we drank our jugs of *chhang*, a fog of mystery would descend on the windy, lamp-lit interiors of the shacks. We would look at the ruddy, weathered faces of the women as they filled our jugs out of the rusty oil-drums in which they brewed the beer, and try to imagine the journey they had made: from their chilly, thin-aired plateau 15,000 feet above sea-level, across the passes of the high Himalayas, down into that steamy slum, floating on a bog of refuse and oil-slicks on the outskirts of Delhi. Everyone who went there got drunk. You couldn't help doing so – it was hard to be in the presence of so terrible a displacement. (16)

Though he is a student when he apparently projects this interpretation onto the life of the serving woman at the Delhi restaurant, his inclusion of the story in this collection of essays tells us a good deal, perhaps, about what becomes a recurring theme in Ghosh's various writings: the "fate" of the migrant in today's world – the migrant intellectual like himself, but even more heartfelt, the fate of the migrant worker in many cultures. "When I next caught the monk's eye," he continues,

> his smile seemed a little guilty: the hospitality of a poor nation must have seemed dispensable compared to the charity of a rich one. Or perhaps he was merely bewildered. It cannot be easy to celebrate the commodification of one's own suffering. (17)

Again, the typical double-edge of a skilled journalist comes to the fore in that passage, in which the double-consciousness of a public representative of a poor but culturally-rich nation like Tibet shines through his placid face.

Granta published the next essay, "Four Corners" in 1988. Set at the intersection of four western American states (New Mexico, Arizona, Colorado, and Utah) it is a starkly beautiful desert region of massive plateaux set on completely flat plains. This is a popular tourist destination in the United States, first for its scenic beauty, and secondly for its importance in Native American history. Ghosh plays on this latter theme, and overlays one of his insistent themes: the notion of borders. Tourists, after all, call this "four corners" because they are told that four states meet in this lunar landscape – though the demarcation is completely invisible and, thus, as good a reminder for Ghosh as any that *all* borders, finally, are arbitrary. "[The tourists] will be back early next morning: the cars and RVs [recreational vehicles] start arriving soon after dawn, their occupants eager to absorb what they can of the magic of the spectacle of two straight lines intersecting" (23). The intersection of space and time fascinates Ghosh again and again in his books. Thus, here, spatially: the four corners, imagined borders between these states; temporally: between Navajos and US colonisers.

The two preceding pieces "were written in the brief hiatus between *The Shadow Lines* and *In An Antique Land*" (vii). The next one, "An Egyptian in Baghdad" appeared in *Granta* in 1990. It was "written in the wake of a deeply disturbing visit to Egypt, shortly before the Gulf War. On returning to the village where I had lived some ten years before – referred to as Nashawy in my later writings on Egypt – I discovered that many of my friends had been trapped on the shores of the Red Sea." He notes that "this piece was to become the basis of the epilogue of *In An Antique Land*" (viii), so it makes an interesting study of how a writer works, how he moves from an early "draft" of sections of a novel, to the finished work. At the end of the essay, he records that

> ...there were more than a dozen of us in the room now. We were crowded around the television set, watching

> carefully, minutely, looking at every face we could see. But there was nothing to be seen except crowds: Nabeel had vanished into the pages of the epic exodus. (45)

But in the "novel" he writes: "Nabeel had vanished into the anonymity of History" (*In An Antique Land:* 353). The "epic exodus" is sharpened into the more strikingly thematic notion of history's anonymous subalterns, the many individuals whose lives are simply not recorded by the powerful. It is an idea to which Ghosh will return again and again.

"The Ghosts of Mrs. Gandhi" was published in *The New Yorker* in 1995, "written in the period between *The Calcutta Chromosome* and *The Glass Palace*" (vii). It provides a powerful account of the riots following Indira Gandhi's assassination. "The targets," writes Ghosh,

> were primarily young Sikhs. They were dragged out, beaten up and then burnt alive. . . . Fires were everywhere; it was the day's motif. Throughout the city, Sikh houses were being looted and then set on fire, often with their occupants still inside. . . . Over the next few days, some twenty-five hundred people died in Delhi alone. Thousands more died in other cities. . . .Entire neighbourhoods were gutted; tens of thousands of people were left homeless. (51-52)

Ghosh records that the one memory that stands out most clearly from that time was the moment when it seemed inevitable that he would be attacked because he was in a group of Hindus protecting their Sikh neighbours. He has many wisely observant things to say in this essay about multi-ethnic, multi-religious societies like India, but he finally turns his attention to the responsibilities of those who record such events. What he says is important to note, beyond the spectacle of the violence, is "the risks that perfectly ordinary people are willing to take for one another" (61). Again, one suspects that for Ghosh it is the "perfectly ordinary" characteristic that is important here, since they and their actions are what is typically *not* paid attention to by journalists and historians. The importance of these riots on Ghosh's own decisions as a writer, especially in his move from *The Circle of Reason* to *The Shadow Lines*, will be discussed in the next chapter.

The next three pieces began as book reviews "but metamorphosed into something less easily defined" (viii): "The Human Comedy in Cairo: a Review of the Work of Naguib Mahfouz" appeared in *The New Republic* in 1990. Having lived in both countries, Ghosh is understandably fascinated by "countries like Egypt and India – old civilisations, trying hard to undo their supersession in the modern world" (64). As we have seen, this is partially the theme of *Countdown*, and is surely at the heart of *In An Antique Land*. Regarding Mahfouz's winning the Nobel Prize, Ghosh writes that

> ... for a prize of such power, the ordinary standards of judgement that apply to books are held in suspension. What matters is that the writer's work be adequately canonical, which is to say, massive, serious, and somehow a part of 'world literature.' If Mahfouz won on these counts, his was the victory of the decathlete, achieved by a slow accumulation of points rather than by a spectacular show of brilliance in a single event. (65)

Maybe Ghosh himself will someday be judged by these same standards. We will wait and see if he has what it takes to become a "decathlete."

"Petrofiction" was published in *The New Republic* in 1992, and again shows his interest in the Indian/African mercantile trade of the Middle Ages. "If the Spice Trade has any twentieth-century equivalent," he writes, "it can only be the oil industry" (75). What this means for a writer is not yet clear, since "the truth is that we do not yet possess the form that can give the Oil Encounter a literary expression" (79). "Empire and Soul: a Review of *The Baburnama*" appeared in *The New Republic* in 1997. His judgement: "*The Baburnama* is the autobiography of India's first Mughal emperor. . . and it is one of the true marvels of the medieval world. . . . the first and until recent times the only true autobiography in Islamic literature" (90).

The next two pieces in the collection "are based on chapters of the thesis for which [he] was awarded a DPhil (PhD) in Social Anthropology by Oxford University in 1982" (viii). Not surprisingly, therefore, their style is markedly different – much more academic, with footnotes and other paraphernalia. "The Relations of Envy", published in *Ethnology* in 1984, is an anthropological study of "the evil eye":

> Envy in Nashawy takes the form it does because the ownership of productive resources is vested in households and because the subdivision of property turns brothers and cousins into competitors in production. On a different scale the same tension lies at the heart of Islamic society . . . it is no coincidence that some egalitarian quasi-socialist movements in the Islamic world are also identified with movements for religious purification. (131)

Such essays remind us of Ghosh's "other" life, the one of a scholar and teacher.

"Categories of Labour and the Orientation of the Fellah Economy" appeared in an anthology entitled *The Diversity of the Muslim Community*, edited by Ahmed al-Shahi in 1987. In it, Ghosh describes the social relationships at the heart of a community of fellahin, and remarks that

> The structure of labour in this community is a means of both resisting and appropriating some of the forms of relationship which have come to be synonymous with 'modernity,' and that finally, the system as a whole constitutes a commentary on the very nature of social relations. (136)

The article was Ghosh's way of "working out why, in this instance, verbs denoting certain calibrations of social relationship superseded verbs that referred to technical acts – an order of precedence that was directly contrary to [his] expectations" (ix). Readers who persevere with these scholarly pieces will discern that, "despite the difference in form and diction, they share with [his] fiction certain characteristic subjects and concerns: most notably [his] interest in *patterns of work* in various societies. It was during [his] stay in Egypt that [he] learnt that even the most mundane forms of labour can embody an entire metaphysic – a discovery that was to have a profound influence on [his] novels *The Circle of Reason* and *The Glass Palace*" (x).

"The Slave of MS. H.6" appeared in *Subaltern Studies*, Vol. 7, in 1992. Robert Dixon comments that

> Ghosh's empirical research can be read as an ethnographic allegory in James Clifford's sense – a form of commentary that uses the past to speak indirectly about the present. His essay in *Subaltern Studies*, 'The Slave of MS.H.6" . . is a remarkably restrained and highly suggestive piece of writing that is surely to be taken as an ironic raspberry blown at the theoretical and critical pretensions of the West. The archive is a synecdoche of postmodernism and

post-modern theoretical practice, with its globalising tendency, and its complicity with the most imperialistic aspects of the modern American state. In Philadelphia, Amitav Ghosh might be travelling *in* the West, but his sly civility ensures that he is not travelling *with* the West. To recover the subaltern consciousness, Ghosh has learned not French but village Arabic; instead of affiliating his text with high theory, he has spent years reading ancient manuscripts and talking to Egyptian peasants. The painstakingly specific and situated nature of his historical research and anthropological inquiry, and the way he has foregrounded his own location, not only in relation to his Egyptian informants but also to the intellectual and military culture of the West, is a challenging model to literary critics in the Western academy whose critical practice involves the application of high theory to Third World texts – we might call *that* 'travelling in the East.' (Robert Dixon 1996: 23)

The next five essays began as lectures. The journal *Public Culture* subsequently published "The Diaspora in Indian Culture" in 1990. In it, Ghosh writes that "the modern Indian diaspora... now represents an important force in world culture [and] is increasingly a factor within the culture of the Indian subcontinent.... To my mind there are no finer writers writing in the English language today than V.S. Naipaul, Salman Rushdie, and A. K. Ramanujan" (243). These are comments that should be kept in mind when we consider Ghosh's placement as an Indian Writing in English, in chapter six. He marvels at "the State's sensitivity to the writing of the diaspora" (244) and provocatively asserts that "the links between India and her diaspora are lived within the imagination" (247). The role of the migrant intellectual in the imagining of the nation (and the writer as imagined by the nation) clearly vexes him. On the one hand, "the institutional relationships between [modern India and its diasporic population], when they exist at all, are all mediated through Britain" (245). On the other hand,

> the opinions of the diaspora are so significant to India: it is that part of itself which is both hostage and representative in the world outside – it is the mirror in which modern India seeks to know itself. (250)

"The Global Reservation" was the Plenary Address at the Annual Meeting of the Society for Cultural Anthropology in 1993, and was subsequently published in *Cultural Anthropology* the following year. "The Fundamentalist Challenge" was published in the *Wilson Quarterly* in 1995. "The March of the Novel Through History" was published in *Kunapipi* and in *The Kenyon Review* in 1998, and it won a Pushcart Prize the following year. Again, his comments on migrancy and the complexity of writing abroad are very pertinent to our discussions in this book. He writes:

> It is the very vastness and cosmopolitanism of the fictional bookcase that requires novelists to locate themselves in relation to it; that demands of their work that it carry marks to establish their location. This then is the peculiar paradox of the novel: those of us who love novels often read them because of the eloquence with which they communicate a 'sense of place.' Yet the truth is that it is the very loss of a lived sense of place that makes their fictional representation possible. (303)

Perhaps this explains a great deal about the preoccupation such writers have with their homeland (think of James Joyce, for example), and the nostalgia that often haunts their works.

The translation of one of Tagore's stories, *Kshudito Pashan*, was published in *Desh* in 1998. "As an allegory of the colonial condition," in Ghosh's opinion, "it is a work of extraordinary suggestive power and atmospheric richness. I finished the translation shortly before I began writing *The Calcutta Chromosome* and it was to have a profound influence on that novel, as well as its successor, *The Glass Palace*" (xii). "The Greatest Sorrow: Times of Joy Recalled in Wretchedness" was the Neelan Thiruchelvam Memorial Lecture for 2001. *Civil Lines* published "The Hunger of Stones" in 1995. Excerpts from "The Ghat of the Only World" were published in *The Nation* in 2002. This was written in memory of a close friend, the poet Agha Shahid Ali, who died on 8 December 2002, and it offers a comment notable both for its poignancy and for its line of reasoning that may remind us of *The Calcutta Chromosome*:

> I could not help myself from wondering whether it was possible that Shahid's identification with his mother was so powerful as to spill beyond the spirit and into the body. Brain cancer is not, so far as I know, a hereditary disease, yet his body had, as it were, elected to reproduce the conditions of his mother's death. But how could this be possible? Even the thought appears preposterous in the bleak light of the Aristotelian distinction between mind and body. (360)

Outside the world of fiction, as we have seen in this chapter, Amitav Ghosh is heavily engaged in the political and cultural wars that shape a postcolonial and globalised world. One cannot pretend that *The Imam and the Indian* is a unified work, since it consists of essays written over a couple of decades. But it does offer a fascinating overview of the many topics that emerge in the fiction that was being written – as if by Ghosh's other hand – while he worked on these prose pieces. It is to those novels that we now turn our attention.

3. A Tale of Two Riots

The Circle of Reason and The Shadow Lines

It follows then that the reason why I – and many others who have written of such events – are compelled to look back in sorrow is because we cannot look ahead. ("The Greatest Sorrow, *The Imam and the Indian:* 317)

The Circle of Reason

Vomited out of their native soil years ago in another carnage, and dumped hundreds of miles away, they had no anger left. Their only passion was memory... Lalpukur could fight no war because it was damned to a hell of longing. (*The Circle of Reason*: 59)

The Story

When he is eight, "Alu" comes to sleepy Lalpukur from Calcutta to live with his uncle Balaram and aunt Toru-debi. He had been given his nickname by his phrenologist uncle, since his large head looked something like a potato and portended an interesting future – at least, so his uncle thought. His parents had recently died in a car accident. Even though Balaram and his brother had been long-estranged, Balaram and Toru-debi decide to take in Alu and raise him, since they had no children of their own. Alu soon displays an amazing ability to pick up various languages. Yet, in one of the many paradoxes that run through the novel, he rarely speaks at all. When at fourteen the boy stops attending school, Balaram, the supposed scientist, surprises everyone by encouraging the boy to take up weaving. Alu begins by taking lessons from Shombhu Debnath, a master weaver. Alu seems a gifted child, just as Balaram had predicted: not only is he good at languages (that he doesn't use), but now he also surpasses his teacher in weaving.

How Balaram became a phrenologist offers us insight into his quirky personality. He had discovered a book on *Practical Phrenology* at a second-hand bookshop in College Street on 11 January, 1950, the day that the physicist Madame Curie was visiting Calcutta. At the time of her visit, Balaram was working for the *Amrita Bazar Patrika* and he went to interview her. As it turns out, he asks what appeared to be a silly question: Madame Curie's hosts had begged off further questions because, they said, she had flown at high altitudes and this had exhausted her. Balaram thinks: "Professor Joliot was wrong; 9000 feet wouldn't tire a Curie. The Curies lived in the highest reaches of the imagination" (16). When his spontaneous observation draws laughter from those at the reception, and then from his workers back at the office, his fragile personality takes a turn that has ramifications for the rest of the story. He decides to leave journalism altogether, and to devote his full energies to phrenology.

The day after the incident at the airport, however, he also accepts an offer of employment from Bhudeb Roy. Roy, a very fat man given to self-aggrandisement, has decided to start a school in remote Lalpukur, about one hundred miles north of Calcutta. Balaram becomes one of his principal teachers. Roy quickly becomes a political bully in the remote village, though, hiring thugs to enforce his policies at the school and elsewhere. The two men become enemies competing for the minds and hearts of the villagers. Sixteen years on, in 1967, Balaram's mind is beginning to show some strain of living under Roy's thumb. He strangely describes the story of his life, for instance, as the biography of the discovery of Reason – but most people around him think he has very little to do with reason; in fact, they find him somewhat comic in his pet notions. He gives them plenty of reason to come to this conclusion: during an especially extravagant puja to Maa Saraswati (goddess of knowledge) planned by Bhudeb Roy to garner favour with the Inspector of Schools, Balaram jumped up onto the statue's platform and ripped off its head, declaring it to be Vanity, rather than Knowledge. In response, Bhudeb Roy surreptitiously poisons the fish in Balaram's pond. Then five of Roy's "sons" attack Balaram's eleven-year-old servant, Maya. In this incident Alu, who was also eleven at the time, had run and fetched Maya's sixteen-year-old brother, who defended her from possible rape.

The next incident in their battle for influence occurs when a plane crashes into Roy's school and burns half of it to the ground. Everyone finds it remarkable that Bhudeb Roy has had the foresight to insure the school just two weeks before the fire, which seems to demonstrate his wisdom, or at least his luck. In response, Balaram seizes upon the destruction to found his own school – much to Bhudeb Roy's chagrin, of course. It is called the Pasteur School of Reason, and is divided into two divisions: in the

Department of Pure Reason, Balaram teaches principles of sanitation; in the Department of Practical Reason, his wife teaches students to tailor and Shombhu Debnath teaches them weaving. Shombhu's son, Rakhal, gives up his revolutionary ways to become the school's business manager. The new school has a very successful first year, so in its second year, a third division is added: the Department of the March of Reason, the home base for Reason Militant. This third division begins by spraying carbolic acid throughout the village, disinfecting everyone and everything. But in the process of this "purification," Balaram completely disrupts Bhudeb Roy's latest political gathering. The next day, Roy burns several of Balaram's possessions to the ground.

Toru-debi responds very negatively to what she considers Balaram's obsessions. After the fish-poisoning, she had taken Balaram's books from their shelves and out into the courtyard, where she sprinkled them with kerosene and burned them all. (Alu, however, had managed to save one book, and presented it to a tearfully grateful Balaram – it was Vallery-Radot's *Life of Pasteur*. This had been the book from which Balaram had read passages to inspire the youthful Alu, and both considered it as sacred as scripture.) Now, after their possessions are burned by Bhudeb Roy, Toru-debi completely loses her mind. Still, Bhudeb Roy is not done with his mischief. He incites Jyoti Das and the police to attack Balaram's compound, and they inadvertently set afire the explosives that Rakhal, the former-revolutionary-turned-business-manager, had resumed making. In the resulting conflagration, Balaram, Toru-debi, Maya, and Rakhal are all killed. In an example of hens coming home to roost, it becomes known that Bhudeb Roy's wife Parboti-debi, who had conceived their daughter on the same night as the plane crash, had actually fathered the job by Shombhu Debnath. Debnath's own wife had died some years after giving birth to Maya. Now, with so much death around them, Shombhu Debnath and Parboti-debi leave with their child and go to Calcutta.

Bhudeb Roy has, thus, set in motion Alu's flight from northern India. The young man is relentlessly pursued by Jyoti Das in a pointless misidentification of "the bad guy" reminiscent of Victor Hugo's *Les Miserables*. Balaram's friend Gopal helps get Alu to Calcutta, where he is introduced to Rajan. Rajan is a member of a caste of weavers that has family connections throughout India. They help him travel down to Kerala and to the small former French-colony of Mahé. All seems fine for a time, but five months after the fire that killed Balaram, Jyoti Das traces Alu to this out-of-the-way spot. However, just two days before, as it happens, Alu had set sail to al-Ghazira with a former prostitute named Zindi al-Tiffaha. She has a house in al-Ghazira in an area called The Severed Head, or the Ras, near the water. There, she takes in all sorts of refugees, some with questionable histories or occupations. Among her current crop, besides Alu, are a Professor Samuel, whose obsession with what he calls the Theory of Queues seems vaguely reminiscent of Balaram's fixation on phrenology and carbolic acid; there's also a young woman named Kulfi, with buck teeth, and apparently recently widowed, and Karthamma, who gives birth to a boy on board, who is named Boss; also, a travelling salesman called Rakesh. When they arrive in al-Ghazira, they meet the rest of the characters in Zindi's little world, including Abu Fahl, who drinks too much; Forid Mian, an old tailor; Jeevanbhai Patel, by far the richest merchant in the area; Hajj Fahmy, a wealthy teetotaller whose family had been among the earliest settlers in the area; handsome Zaghloul the Pigeon; and Mast Ram, who falls in love with Kulfi. When she does not return the favour, Mast Ram, in a scene reminiscent of the burning of Balaram's school, commits suicide and in the process sets fire to the village, burning 50 shacks to the ground.

Somehow, a massive building called "The Star" collapses and traps Alu in a very narrow furrow beneath the heaps of concrete. Strangely, as if his aunt were looking out for him from on high, two Singer sewing machines prop the concrete slab up. Most think Alu is dead. When he is freed after a few days he emerges a new man, almost a reincarnation of Gandhi – or, at least, of Balaram:

> He was sitting behind the loom on the platform, weaving very fast, but without so much as looking at the loom, and talking all the while. And in a way that was the strangest thing of all; that he was talking. For Alu was a very silent man. (278)

He begins immediately speaking about "cleanliness and dirt and the Infinitely Small" (235) – and about Louis Pasteur. More disturbingly, perhaps, he speaks about the need for a war against money. He wins converts to his cause, and the result will remind readers of Balaram's earlier school: a communistic system in which all salaries are pooled and no one makes a profit from their enterprise beyond what they immediately need.

Meanwhile, we turn our attention to Zindi and her circle of supporters. Alu's mystical renunciation of profit sends Zindi into paroxysms of concern, since she has hoarded money for years and years. She now sees her financial security threatened by the very people she has helped for so many years, so she seeks another kind of protection. She angles to get Jeevanbhai Patel's shop from him by trying to get Forid Mian to marry her, but Jeevanbhai commits suicide just before her plan is to come to fruition. Though it is not made explicit, it seems that for some time Jeevanbhai had been acting as a spy for the local magistrate. Through the magistrate, Jeevanbhai has betrayed Alu to Jyoti Das.

Echoing the conflagration in which he had destroyed Balaram's world, Jyoti Das and the local magistrate bring down the power of the law on a gathering of those who subscribe to Alu's communist doctrine. Many are killed in the fire, just as many had been in Balaram's: Hajj Fahmy, Rakesh, and Karthamma. Once again, a migration is called for. Zindi leads Alu, Kulfi, the baby Boss, Abu Fahl, and Zaghloul, to her native village. But instead of finding refuge there, her family rejects them – even though it had been her money over the years that had built homes for her brothers and their wives. We learn that she had been abandoned long ago by her husband in Alexandria, when it was discovered that she was barren. So now Zindi and company head further west to Algeria. All along their trip, though, they are dogged by Jyoti Das still in pursuit.

In Algeria, Zindi has Alu and Kulfi pretend to be married, and they call themselves Mr. and Mrs. Bose. In this new setting, we are introduced to a small emigrant Indian community: Mr. and Mrs. Verma, Dr. and Mrs. Mishra, and Miss Krishnaswamy, a nurse. Dr. Uma Verma, "a short, pleasantly plump, honey-complexioned woman in her mid-thirties" (355), is a microbiologist, and daughter of Hem Narain Mathur. Dr. Mishra is a surgeon. His father had been Maithili Sharan Mishra, who had espoused fashionable socialism after attaining his degree from the

London School of Economics, but who had grown fat on various governmental ministerial positions. The "real" socialist, Hem Narain Mathur, had meanwhile sunk into obscurity.

It turns out, however, that Jyoti Das is a house guest of the Mishra's, and he inevitably meets Alu and friends. Jyoti Das, still a virgin, begs Kulfi for one night's liaison – and at the suggestion she has a heart attack and dies. An argument ensues between Verma and Mishra over the possibilities of performing a proper Hindu funeral for her. In his conversation with Jyoti Das, Alu learns more of what happened when he and Zindi managed to escape the ambush of the protesters at the Star. Hajj Fahmy, Professor Samuel, Chunni, Rakesh and many of the others had not died but had been deported to Egypt or India. Hajj Fahmy died of shock that same day, though. Meanwhile, the Professor still held out hope for the future, suggesting that "the queue of hopes stretches long past infinity" (409). Alu, Zindi and the baby, Boss, continue their migration west, at least as far as Tangier, where they bid Jyoti Das farewell as he heads to a new life in Europe. They then turn happily back towards al-Ghazira.

Themes and Concerns

The emotional quote about Lalpukur that opened our discussion of *The Circle of Reason* suggests that its author feels very deeply indeed, about history's victims – especially those who are forced into exile by events beyond their control. This first of Ghosh's novels is a complex tapestry of stories of individuals whose lives overlap, pull apart, and separate – and sometimes find each other again in new contexts. It is a story of obsession – obsessive rationalism that some embrace as science and others ridicule as insanity (the science of "queues" and purification by carbolic acid), and obsessive manhunts. The book is an early example of this novelist's tendency to push against the limits of a particular genre: after all, *The Circle of Reason* is, at once, a detective story, a story of exile, a travelogue, a women's rights tract, a Marxist protest, a plea for humanistic camaraderie, etc. The narrative techniques employed here sometimes share the characteristics of magical realism (Toru-debi, for example, strangely looks upon her Singer sewing machine as her child), but they are more generally straightforward and realistic. He does tend, though, to juggle a lot of characters, time zones, and locales in the telling of his tale.

A recurring pattern in the novel is the "chance" destruction rained down upon many others by the actions of a few. But Ghosh uses narration as the thread that will weave these chance events into a pattern – across continents and across time – as if the weird logic that guides Balaram is akin to that of a storyteller, theologian, or philosopher who *will* find a meaningful pattern in the world. Alu, his protégé, eventually learns to "weave the world" in complex patterns that somehow express metaphysical meaning. In his bizarre giftedness he challenges Shombhu, his teacher, who had despaired long ago of ever again finding meaning or joy in life. In fact, in a self-destructive move, he cynically destroys Alu's most ambitious philosophical weaves. One might see here a foreshadowing of the book's later debate between Mrs. Verma and the cynical Dr. Mishra. The book asks us to consider types of knowledge and avenues whereby patterns of meaning may manifest themselves

A Tale of Two Riots

to us through time. Is it all "chance," or is it a tapestry that has a method behind apparent madness? Step back far enough from history and can we see the "weave"?

Take the case of Balaram. He turned to phrenology, he said, because this appeared to him to be a field of study that bridged science with personality:

> Don't you see? said Balaram, . . . In this science the inside and the outside, the mind and the body, what people do and what they are, are *one*. Don't you see how *important* it is? (17)

From that moment on, he began discovering meaningful bumps on heads that confirmed the very personality traits that he had observed in the individuals – the "science" of phrenology seemed a case of a self-fulfilling prophecy, in other words. But such ridiculous characters are often dear to their creator's heart, and we must wonder if Balaram has a family resemblance to Shakespeare's Polonius (in *Hamlet*), speaking more wisdom than his silliness might lead us to believe.

In college, Balaram and two of his friends, Dantu and Gopal, had started an organisation called – again, with some irony – the Rationalists. They proposed to find universal principles of reason to explain all phenomena, just as Balaram's later interest in the dubious science of phrenology purported to do. In fact, as the book progresses, Balaram seems increasingly reminiscent of Voltaire's character in *Candide*, Pangloss, who reads all evidence through his own rose-coloured glasses. Thus, when the plane crashed into Bhudeb Roy's school, burning more than half of it to the ground, Balaram argues that "if it has no meaning, why would it happen? Of course it has a meaning, but the meaning must be read rationally" (86). Far more pragmatic, his friend Gopal concludes that "Chance doesn't have a meaning – that's why it's chance" (90). Whom are we to believe: Balaram, Alu, and Mrs. Verma, or Gopal, Dr. Mishra, and Jyoti Das?

By "chance," Mrs. Verma's father was Hem Narain Mathur – Dantu's real name. This "apostate" Rationalist had gone on to become an agitator for landless labourers in north Bihar. Mathur (Dantu) had been guided by the *Life of Pasteur* that his friend, Balaram, had entrusted to him so many years before, the same book from which Balaram had read to the young Alu. When Alu discovers the book on his bookshelf in Algeria – by chance – he admits its importance in his upbringing to Mrs. Verma and describes it as his "only real brother" (395). She, in turn, admits that it was this very book that determined her vocation as a microbiologist, and she returns the book to Alu as if he were its rightful owner and she was closing a circle. Discovering that their fathers had been college friends, Alu and Mrs. Verma seem almost like cousins to each other – family members who discover each other, willy-nilly, halfway around the world. When Alu and Kulfi adopt the pseudonym of Mr. and Mrs. Bose, at Zindi's urging, we recall that Bose had been Balaram's last name – underscoring the book's suggestion of reincarnation, or at least continuity throughout generations.

Exile is another theme touched upon in this novel, and then returned to with more emphasis in Ghosh's later work. At the book's end it is the "villain," Jyoti Das, who becomes the full-fledged migrant, now finding himself forever on the run. Ghosh had foreshadowed Jyoti Das' fate much earlier in the book when he had him reflect as follows:

> Foreign places are all alike in that they are not home. Nothing binds you there.... He knew that his swimming head had no connection with that hint of sand in the distance. It would have made no difference whether that bit of land was al-Ghazira or Antarctica. The journey was within and it was already over, for the most important thing was leaving. (266)

Alu, on the other hand, has found a new community with Zindi and seeks a new rootedness-in a foreign land, to be sure, but with a sense of new connection.

The dichotomy between the chance of reason and the "story" of connection takes on a political edge when, in something of a set piece, Ghosh portrays an exilic Indian community in this novel. Though few in number, they are sharply drawn and displayed as being at each others' throats, vying for authenticity as *the* spokesperson for an "authentic" Indian culture. In this regard, Mrs. Verma decidedly gets the better of the argument – expressing a sincere appreciation of Hinduism, for example, while Dr. Mishra seems completely deracinated. The ironies mount up, as they propose to put on a tableau vivant of the tale of Chitrangada and Arjuna, with Kulfi, former prostitute, as the heroine. Dr. Mishra clearly knows the detailed rubrics involved in Hindu rituals, but he has not imbibed its true spirit. His hardened cynicism is countered by Mrs. Verma's humility and simple clinging to truth. Against the jaded Dr. Mishra's hypocritical insistence on rubric propriety, Mrs. Verma embraces syncretism:

> He nodded weakly. The world has come full circle, he groaned. Carbolic acid has become holy water.... The times are like that, Mrs. Verma said sadly. Nothing's whole any more. If we wait for everything to be right again, we'll wait for ever while the world falls apart.

> The only hope is to make do with what we've got.
> (411-12, 416-17)

Thus, since they do not have water from the Ganges to purify the body and the burial site, Mrs. Verma uses carbolic acid that recurs throughout the story with unnerving regularity. When Dr. Mishra responds that he thinks she is being remarkably irrational for a microbiologist, Mrs. Verma eschews her science in favour of a sort of mysticism, wondering whether or not the microbes under the scientist's microscope are, in fact, "a bodily metaphor for human pain and unhappiness and perhaps joy as well." But this sort of musing, she admits, is an activity that scientists will not allow themselves to consider (412). She, herself, has no such hesitation. "[I]f there's one thing people learn from the past," she remarks, somewhat mysteriously, "it is that every consummated death is another beginning" (414). Alu joins with her in this religious conclusion, solemnly adding the *Life of Pasteur* to the funeral pyre as if certain that it, also, will be reborn.

In Chapter One, we took note of Ghosh's comments on his own narrative technique and on how he prefers to move from the external to the internal, from the physical to its impact on one's interior sense of identity. This desire to blur the distinction between the external and the interior, the physical and the mental, recurs with special significance in *The Calcutta Chromosome*, the novel that takes up Ghosh's interest in science where *The Circle of Reason* leaves off.

Let us close our discussion of this novel with a brief reference to a theme only touched upon in *The Circle of Reason* but taken up with more insistence in *The Shadow*

A Tale of Two Riots

Lines. This is what might best be suggested by a question: "Whose history are we referring to when we speak of History?" Balaram offers us a clue. As a student, he had been fascinated by science, but his teachers forced him to get a degree in history. His mind therefore tended to merge the two subjects and to emphasise those events that advanced scientific knowledge:

> He had his own version of Calcutta. For him it was the city in which Ronald Ross discovered the origin of malaria, and Robert Koch, after years of effort, finally isolated the bacillus which causes typhoid. It was the Calcutta in which Jagadish Bose first demonstrated the extraordinarily life-like patterns of stress responses in metals; where he first proved to a disbelieving world that plants are no less burdened with feeling than man. (41)

Notice that politics does not enter into Balaram's notion of the history of Calcutta. What Ghosh is reminding us, clearly, is that there is much that goes on that is never recorded or, if recorded, is nonetheless ignored. He is fond of occasionally suggesting "alternate" histories – by which I do not mean "what if?" scenarios, but rather a reinterpretation or re-emphasising of things that actually *did* take place but were not deemed significant enough for posterity's notice. Sometimes, this means viewing history "from below" – as recorded by non-Europeans, for example – rather than from imperial heights. The "Indian" version of 1914 that Balaram offers early in the novel is one stunning example (in Chapter Two, "A Pasteurised Cosmos," 39), and another is a brief revisionist history of cotton – which concludes: "Every scrap of cloth is stained by a bloody past" (56-58). Whose blood, one may ask. Ghosh, surely, would have us do so.

The Shadow Lines

"Looking back today, it strikes me that *The Circle of Reason* could . . . be identified as an exodus novel, a story of migration in the classic sense of having its gaze turned firmly towards the future. . . . I was working on the last part of the book in 1984 when the riots broke out . . . .[T]he violence had the effect of bringing to the surface of my memory events from my own childhood, when I had indeed been in a similar situation." (Ghosh, "The Greatest Sorrow," *The Imam .and the Indian*: 314)

> . . . *The Shadow Lines* . . . became a book not about any one event but about the meaning of such events and their effects on the individuals who live through them. . . . I had to resolve a dilemma, between being a writer and being a citizen. ("The Ghosts of Mrs. Gandhi," *The Imam and the Indian:* 60, 61)

The Story

The time sequence in the story is jumbled: the crucial events occur in the 1960's, but the narrator is recalling them in the 1980's, and they are "rooted" in the period just before the First World War. Thus, in 1939, thirteen years before the narrator was born, his twenty-nine-year-old great aunt, Mayadebi, went to England along with her husband and their son, Tridib. In later years, she always had the aura of a movie star for the narrator, someone a bit larger than life who had seen the world. She was his grandmother's only sister. His grandmother never approved of Tridib, whom she considered lazy – and in her opinion, wasted time soon begins to stink. The narrator disagreed with his grandmother's estimation, since he loved Tridib's healthy imagination that resulted in an endless supply of stories that never allowed time to "stink" – and Tridib took ample advantage of the narrator's youthful tendency toward gullibility. Tridib had two brothers. One was two years older, frequently away since he worked for the United Nations. His name was Jatin. The other brother was much younger, named Robi. Tridib was the only one of the three who had spent much of his life in Calcutta, living in the sprawling old family house in Ballygunge Place with grandmother. The narrator thought that his grandmother didn't just disapprove of Tridib, but actually feared him.

Mrs. Price, her daughter May, and her son Nick, lived in north London. Her husband, who had been one of her college teachers, had recently died. As it happens, Mrs. Price's father, Lionel Tresawsen, had been stationed in India when she was young, and he had become a good friend of Tridib's grandfather, who was a judge in the Calcutta High Court. The narrator met May when she came to India for a visit some years later, and then did not see her for another seventeen years, when he returned the favour and visited England. He was, at that later period, spending a year in London doing research at the India Office Library for a PhD thesis on the textile trade between India and England in the nineteenth century. By that time, May had become a cellist in an orchestra, but when she had visited India, she had just been learning the basics. When he attended one of her concerts, they began a friendship, and she filled in many of the details of her life that the narrator had been wondering about all those years. She noted, for example, that in 1959, when she was nineteen and Tridib was twenty-seven, they had begun a long correspondence. He had been sending her family. Christmas cards ever since he had left London in 1940, but now he began writing specifically to her alone.

Ila is the narrator's cousin, just a few years older than he. As the daughter of Jatin, the diplomat, she has travelled widely and seen a lot of the world, and she lives very decidedly in the present. She's more sophisticated than the narrator, even a bit jaded, but is more than a little insecure in her personal relationships. She marries Nick and lives in Mrs. Price's house in London, but the narrator picks up tensions between Ila and her philandering husband. Some years earlier, Nick had not defended Ila in an incident at school when she was ridiculed; in fact, he had left early to avoid being seen with her. Desperately proud, Ila tries to cover up the story.

He goes back to Delhi to take his University examinations, since his grandmother's condition had improved a bit. But she dies in Calcutta in his absence and is cremated, and he feels guilty: "she had always been too passionate a person to find a real place in my tidy late-bourgeois world, the world that I had inherited, in which examinations were more important than death" (90). Near her death, his grandmother correctly surmises that he had visited prostitutes in Delhi, and she passes the information along to his dean. In order to save his academic career, he denies the accusation. He marvels at his grandmother's vindictiveness, but also at her uncanny knowledge. Part One ("Going Away") ends with the narrator looking back eighteen years, when Ila went away to London for University even though she knew he loved her, and thereby "wrenched [him] into adulthood by demonstrating for the first time, and for ever the inequality of [their] needs" (110).

A Tale of Two Riots

Part Two (Coming Home) begins in 1962, a momentous year for the narrator's family. It was the year the narrator turned ten, the year his father became General Manager of his firm, the year his grandmother retired as headmistress at a girls' school where she had spent twenty-seven years. In a year or two, his grandmother gradually receded to her room, where she began sharing her memories of her girlhood home in Dhaka. Grandmother tells the narrator how she had eventually married an engineer and spent the first twelve years of her marriage "in a succession of railway colonies in towns with fairy-tale names like Moulmein and Mandalay.... [but] to her, nothing ... in that enchanted pagoda-land had seemed real enough to remember" (122). In this, as we shall see, she is remarkably like Ila. The narrator's father had been born in Mandalay in 1925, and grandmother took him back to Dhaka once a year. But when he was six, grandmother's parents both died. The narrator's father and grandmother seldom visited Dhaka again, but stayed in Mandalay. In 1935, grandfather died of pneumonia when grandmother was just thirty-two. After Partition, she had never returned to the city. She used her degree in history from Dhaka University to get a teaching job.

But in 1964, by chance, grandmother meets up with a poor distant relation who lives near a dump, and learns that her family house in Dhaka is now occupied only by grandmother's uncle, Jethamoshai, who is now over ninety, and by Muslim refugees from India. Her sister Maya had moved to Dhaka when her husband had become Councillor in the Deputy High Commission there, and so grandmother decides to take this occasion to visit Maya and to bring Jethamoshai back to India. This decision startles everyone: his grandmother "had never pretended to have much family feeling; she had always founded her morality, schoolmistress-like, in larger and more abstract entities" (127). Something is calling her back to that split house, in a desperate last-minute attempt at reconciliation and wholeness.

She goes on the third of January, 1964. The narrator is eleven at the time. Tridib decides to accompany grandmother and to bring along May Price, who had been visiting him from England. The trip is momentous for everyone. Jethamoshai, when they find him, doesn't want to go with them back to India:

> Once you start moving you never stop. That's what I told my sons when they took the trains. I said: I don't believe in this India-Shindia. It's all very well, you're going away now, but suppose when you get there they decide to draw another line somewhere? What will you do then? Where will you move to? No one will have you anywhere. As for me, I was born here, and I'll die here. (211)

But they manage to get him in the car, and attempt to leave. They soon find, however, that their way is blocked by a mob. May urges Tridib to get out of the car and retrieve Jethamoshai, who had wandered into the mob. When he tries to do so, Tridib is overcome by the mob and killed. After Tridib's death, the narrator is sent to stay with his mother's brother in Durgapur; Tridib is cremated, and May leaves for London that same day; Mayadebi and her family return to Dhaka.

Themes and Concerns

The Shadow Lines deals with the effects of fear on memory and one's engagement with the world. The memories of the 1964 riot traumatise the narrator, and he successfully blocks them until a chance remark that he overhears during the 1984 riots prompts a personal crisis and a detailed unpacking of the earlier trauma. As he recounts the events, he recalls snippets of conversations with relatives and friends that suggest that they, too, had been redefined by their experiences that day. In her conversations with him seventeen years after the actual events, for example, May Price looks back, still wondering if she had visited India when she did because she was in fact in love with Tridib – and she still cannot answer her question. "I don't know whether everything else that happened was my fault: whether I'd have behaved otherwise if I'd really loved him" (172). The plot of this novel engages readers and deeply resonates for many Indians, Pakistanis, and Bangladeshis. Anyone reading the novel, though, will recognise that its impact can be attributed more to the *manner* of the telling than to the recitation of the events themselves. The Partition, after all, has been the subject of several very good novels. As Suvir Kaul puts it, though,

> the pressure of this question – do you remember – generates the form of the novel: its partial answers, its digressions, its looping, non-linear, wide-ranging narrative technique . . . for *The Shadow Lines* is an archaeology of silences, a slow brushing away of some of the cobwebs of modern Indian memory, a repeated return to those absences and fissures that mark the sites of personal and national trauma. (Suvir Kaul, 1994: 126).

Kaul wisely broadens the narrator's experience and makes it India's, for this is not simply a *Bildungsroman*, a story of one young man's coming of age. It is, rather, one man's embodiment of the "national trauma" that lives on in the lives of today's South Asians. What Ghosh has done in such a masterly fashion is to find an apt *process* for demonstrating the neurosis that has resulted. One thinks of T.S. Eliot's nervous breakdown, coupling personal problems with the effects of a World War, and his fragmentary masterpiece, *The Wasteland* (1922), that seeks a means to embody the poet's desire to piece himself and his culture back together. Like that collection of the shards of a poet's memory, *The Shadow Lines* in a non-sequential and hesitant journey back and forth to the centre of the trauma – the murder of his uncle – that is as remarkable for its psychological sophistication as for the resulting novel's complex theme. It is as much about how the imagination works in managing one's memories as it is about the arbitrary nature of nations and borders, but in *The Shadow Lines*, Ghosh has found a wonderful vehicle to merge the two ideas.

Ghosh is fascinated by the interaction of Space and Time, and his narrator is fascinated throughout the novel with the impact that a particular place – an alleyway, a darkened living room – can have on one particular individual, while others pass it by unscathed. Ila would *appear* to be in the latter category, whereas the narrator is very much susceptible to the connotations of place. One of the reasons, in fact, that his uncle Tridib's death has had such a traumatising impact on the narrator's memory is that "Tridib had given [him] worlds to travel in and he had given [him] eyes to see them with" (20). No one had done this for Ila, and she was therefore simply set adrift in an undifferentiated world without an imaginative map to interpret what she was seeing. Ila, writes the narrator, "who had been travelling around the world since she was a child, could never understand what those hours in Tridib's room had meant to me, a boy who had never been more than a few hundred miles from Calcutta" (20). When the narrator visited her in London, it was as though he had just stepped into the set of his favourite film: he marvelled at everything that made Tridib's stories concrete – but Ila simply grew impatient: "I could not persuade her that a place does not merely exist, that it had to be invented in one's imagination . . . . so that although she had lived in many places, she had never travelled at all" (21). What he most admired in his uncle was this gift: "the one thing he wanted to teach me, he used to say, was to use my imagination with precision" (24).

Much like Wordsworth, for Tridib, an experience was fine when it happened, but it became more wonderful and potentially *meaningful* when it was re-lived in the imagination. But for Ila, "the current was the real: it was as though she lived in a present which was like an airlock in a canal, shut away from the tidewaters of the past and the future by steel floodgates" (30). She had, as it were, no sense of history. She had no connection with the person she *once* was, and was consequently very unsure of where she was headed.

> Tridib. . . had said that we could not see without inventing what we saw, so at least we could try to do it properly. And then, because she shrugged dismissively and said: Why? Why should we try, why not just take the world as it is? I told her how he had said that we had to try because the alternative wasn't blankness – it only meant that if we didn't try ourselves, we would never be free of other people's inventions. (31)

This of course has ramifications in grandmother's story, as we shall see, and in those of anyone affected by Partition; but one might see the implications for someone like Ila, as well, in the world that was "imagined" for her by Nick and others like him: they gave her a cramped world, despite her travels.

The narrator is like his uncle, in the long run – very much alive to the place in which he is living, and alert to the potential emergence of other places in his imagination. Even more than his uncle, though, he is sensitive to the *history* of a place. Having read his novels, it is not surprising to learn that Ghosh himself was first a student of history in college. We hear that younger self speaking in this slight break in the flow of his narrative:

> There is nothing quite as evocative as an old newspaper. There is something in its urgent contemporaneity – the weather reports, the lists of that day's engagements in the city, the advertisements for half-remembered films, still crying out in bold print as though it were all happening *now*, today – and the feeling besides that one may once have handled, if not that very paper, then its exact likeness, its twin, which transports one in time as nothing else can. (222)

As far as the narrative itself is concerned, it takes on the characteristics of a palimpsest, with incidents from the past bleeding through to the present. Under Tridib's tutelage (and, inadvertently, under Ila's, as well – recall that they had spent many days as children hiding and imagining unseen rooms,) he has become a walking tour guide for particular streets and houses in London, even before visiting them.

It is clear that the narrator valorises Tridib's sense of adventure in imagining places in *time as well as in space*, and he underscores what Ila has lost in her insistence on a flat immediacy of experience. But the book does not end

A Tale of Two Riots

there, for it is equally interested in exploring the problematic nature of the projections that Tridib's imaginative trips evoke in the narrator. Grandmother is offered as a case in point. When she finally makes the momentous trip back to Dhaka, she refuses to believe that she is, in fact, *there*.

> The Dhaka she was thinking of was the city that had surrounded their old house.... I could see all that, because people like my grandmother, who have no home but in memory, learn to be very skilled in the art of recollection. (190)

It is not until the car turns down her old street that her memories fall into place and the present can *intersect* the past. As they approach her old house in Dhaka, grandmother becomes very alert, looking for familiar landmarks, "Kana-babu's sweet-shop" (202), "the lime trees her mother had once planted" (204).

Most people have such experiences, and they are harmless. More troublesome, though, are the many passages in the book that ponder the meaning of borders between countries, and between individuals, which are described as similarly flawed imaginative projections. Grandmother is rightly *mystified* by the notion of borders. "But if there aren't any trenches or anything," she asks the others in the car,

> how are people to know? I mean, where's the difference then? And if there's no difference, both sides will be the same; it'll be just like it used to be before, when we used to catch a train in Dhaka and get off in Calcutta the next day without anybody stopping us. What was it all for then – Partition and all the killing and everything – if there isn't something in between? (149)

Looking back on the situation, the narrator recalls he laughed hysterically at her confusion. But he was no longer laughing when he looked back on the trip where it happened. He realises that "she liked things to be neat and in place – and at that moment she had not been able quite to understand how her place of birth had come to be so messily at odds with her nationality" (149). The narrator marvels that people invest such *power* in the lines of maps. He recognises in this mania for, definition of who "we" are, a horrible irony that had led to his uncle's brutal death: "each city [Dhaka and Calcutta] was the inverted image of the other, locked into anx irreversible symmetry by the line that was to set us free – our looking-glass border" (228).

Looking across the imagined border between India and East Pakistan, what you see is something exactly like yourself. In fact, what you see is something that was, in fact, you.

The residue of history in space – the detritus of wars and empires. Tridib's brother Robi later puts the question in angry terms: "why don't they draw thousands of little lines through the whole subcontinent and give every little place a new name? What would it change? It's a mirage; the whole thing is a mirage" (241). And despite his fascination with atlases, real and imaginary, it does take the narrator quite a while to face the arbitrary horrors that his grandmother saw so honestly on the spot. As if to tie this book to his first one, Ghosh has his narrator draw a circle on a map – though not, perhaps, a circle of "reason" – with Khulna at its centre and Srinagar on its circumference. He notes that

> ...Hanoi and Chungking are nearer Khulna than Srinagar, and yet did the people of Khulna care at all about the fate of the mosques in Vietnam and South China (a mere stone's throw away)? I doubted it: (227)

A Tale of Two Riots

The implied question here – whose *nation*? – leads the reader inevitably to Ghosh's enduring question: whose *history*? This is the subject of the biggest argument between the narrator and Ila, in which she praises the Marxist students with whom she is living because

> ...we may not achieve much in our little house in Stockwell, but we *know* that in the future political people everywhere will look to us – in Nigeria, India, Malaysia, wherever.... You wouldn't understand the exhilaration of events like that – nothing really important ever happens where you are. (102)

The narrator is furious, but not particularly eloquent in what he shouts back. Years later, though, in reflecting over the experience, he can have the last word: "She seemed immeasurably distant then, in her serene confidence in the centrality and eloquence of her experience, in her quiet pity for the pettiness of lives like mine, lived out in the silence of voiceless events in a backward world" (102). Yet, Ila's Marxist friends relegate her to a stereotype, and in the process denigrate her as she now denigrates her cousin. Her life is surely no more important than the narrator's. She triumphantly accuses the narrator of knowing nothing about England, and he admits she is correct. He adds, ironically, "I knew nothing at all about England except as an invention" (103).

In the end, though the narrator's experiences may resonate in the lives of many readers, this is a personal story. These are individuals who share a history of a particular trauma, one that marked them indelibly. As it happens, it arose from and now signifies that larger national trauma that is called the Partition, but it is first and foremost lived by the particular individuals that Ghosh remembers. Thus, a psychologist might suggest that their central trauma is "remembered" first by their bodies:

> We were stupefied with fear . . .It is a fear that comes of the knowledge that normalcy is utterly contingent, that the spaces that surround one, the streets that one inhabits, can become, suddenly and without warning, as hostile as a desert in a flash flood. It is this that sets apart the thousand million people who inhabit the subcontinent from the rest of the world – not language, not food, not music – it is the special quality of loneliness that grows out of the fear of the war between oneself and one's image in the mirror. (200)

Who are we? Who do we dream of being? The image that took the place of Nick Price's face in the narrator's mirror some fifteen years later – after he had come to terms with 1964 – may still not have come into sharp focus.

We need to ask one more "personal" question before we move to another thematic issue, and that has to do with the hero of the tale: Tridib. What are we to think of him? Years later, May Price concludes that she had not, in fact, been responsible for his death, though it had been a question that had plagued her: "He gave himself up" she tells the narrator seventeen years after the event. "It was a sacrifice. I know I can't understand it, I know I mustn't try, for any real sacrifice is a mystery" (246). It seemed somehow uncharacteristic of him, a surprise to the reader, when Tridib suddenly hops out of the car and enters the mob. He has been the man who lives in the imagination, the favourite uncle who tells a good yarn. In fact, as a young man the narrator is often taken in by him.

> Tridib laughs and shakes me by the neck and tells me . . .
> Everyone lives in a story, he says, my grandmother, my father, *his* father, Lenin, Einstein, and lots of other names

A Tale of Two Riots

> I hadn't heard of; they all lived in stories, because stories are all there are to live in, it was just a question of which one you choose. (179)

And Tridib, according to May, seems to have chosen to live the story of Tristan, "a very sad story, about a man without a country, who fell in love with a woman-across-the-seas" (183). But it is this man who lives in stories who uncharacteristically walks toward the very real mob.

Perhaps May is the one living that particular dream in which Tridib becomes "Tristan." When she received her fourth letter from him, he had told her that he wanted to meet her

> . . .in a place without a past, without history, free, really free, two people coming together with the utter freedom of strangers. But of course, if that was to happen, she would have to come to India. They would find a place like that somewhere. (141)

The absurdity of finding such a place in India is manifest, and the narrator describes the letter with an interesting adjective: he calls it pornographic. On one level, this is surely attributable to its sexual content, but on a broader thematic level I would suggest that the pornographic notion is the letter's expressed desire for a *lack of history*. This may have been May's dream – travelling off to India to meet her exotic prince – but it is more accurately described as Tridib's temptation. She is right about one thing, in stepping out of the car to intervene in history, he *has* made a sacrifice.

Some two hundred million years ago, Antarctica was joined to South America, Africa, India, and Australia in a single large continent called Gondwanaland. What Tridib most desires, it seems, would be a leap over the arbitrary borders and distinctions and consequent rivalries and hatreds that have accumulated with history, and return somehow to a truer sense of commonality. As Suvir Kaul puts it,

> Tridib's yearning, addressed to a time and space before subcontinental borders, before the historical alienation of culture and self, exists as an unqualified, untrammelled, trace memory of psychic wholeness and identity. Such desire can of course only exist prior to historical or geographical calculation, and is manifestly unrealisable. In its function as critique and as utopian hope, however, it is quite as real as the shadow-lines that mock the limits of our political consciousness and imagination.(Suvir Kaul: 142)

But to live in that dream is to step outside history. Tridib's heroism, therefore, was to recognise the absurdity of history, and to step into the melee nonetheless.

How had he come to this choice? Early in the novel, possibly unnoticed as we try to piece together the narrator's memories for him, Tridib had addressed the issue of the intersection of the personal with the historical. He refused to be overcome by life's fragility. For him, personal relationships must be definitive, even if they are fleeting. Here is that meditation: it is wartime in London; he is walking down a street with some friends, and he thinks to himself:

> ...even walking down that street, that evening, they knew what was coming – not the details, nor the timing perhaps, but they knew, all four of them, that their world, and in all probability they themselves, would not survive the war. ... And in the meanwhile, there they are, in that gilded summer, laughing and singing on their way back to Brick Lane. (66-67)

Twenty-five years later, he steps out of a car in Dhaka and is slaughtered by a mob whipped into frenzy by their imagined notions of nation.

The Shadow Lines is a very different book and a surprise after *The Circle of Reason*. Ghosh alters his writing agenda and his style after 1984 because the riots in *The Shadow Lines* emerge from the author's memory only *after* the riots of 1984. Regarding the communal rioting in Srinagar, Calcutta and Dhaka in 1964, the narrator of *The Shadow Lines* remarks that "It actually took me *fifteen years* to discover that there was a connection between my nightmare bus ride back from school and the events that befell Tridib and the others in Dhaka. . . . I believed in the reality of nations and borders." (214). As in *The Circle of Reason*, we see Ghosh's fascination with chance, reminiscent of the chance memory that launched the author's literary hero, Marcel Proust, into his vast autobiographical novel *Remembrance of Things Past*.

For Proust a very long chain of memories had been suddenly triggered by the taste of a particular cookie dipped in tea, a taste that reminded him of his grandmother's house, his father's death, and everything else. So too with Ghosh:

> *The Circle of Reason* had grown upwards, like a sapling rising from the soil of my immediate experience; *The Shadow Lines* had its opening planted in the present, but it grew downwards, into the soil, like a root system straining to find a source of nourishment. It was in this process that I came to examine the ways in which my own life had been affected by civil violence. I remembered stories my mother had told me about the Great Calcutta Killing of 1946; I remembered my uncles' stories of anti-Indian riots in Rangoon in 1930 and 1938. At the heart of

> the book, however, was an event that had occurred in Dhaka in 1964, the year before my family moved to Colombo: in the unlit depths of my memory there stirred a recollection of a night when our house, flooded with refugees, was besieged by an angry mob. I had not thought of this event in decades, but after 1984 it began to haunt me . . . I went to libraries and sifted through hundreds of newspapers and in the end, through perseverance, luck and guesswork I did find out what had happened. The riots of my memory were not a local affair: they had engulfed much of the subcontinent. ("The Greatest Sorrow," *The Imam and the Indian* :315)

One of the wonders of *The Shadow Lines* is the technique that Ghosh has found to demonstrate the confusion from which his memories slowly, piece by piece, come to the surface and gradually coalesce. The reader is made to experience the process along with the narrator, in a book that is anything but linear.

The first half of *The Shadow Lines* is titled "Going Away," and the second half is "Coming Home." *Where* that home might be is the question haunting all of Ghosh's subsequent writing. The depth of that uncertainty can be felt in his description of the incident in which Nick deserts young Ila to her persecutors at school. The narrator is relentless in his analysis of his cousin, observing her with heartfelt clarity:

> Ila walking alone in a drizzle under that cold grey sky: Ila who in Calcutta was surrounded by so many relatives and cars and servants . . . Ila walking alone because Nick Price was ashamed to be seen by his friends, walking home with an Indian. (75)

She is, perhaps, the most conflicted character in the book-barring the narrator himself. As Suvir Kaul astutely notes,

"Ila functions very much as the narrator's double, her likeness close enough for her differences to cause him to reflect upon himself" (129). But how she resembles him is the interesting part of the equation, especially if Kaul is correct in noting that *"The Shadow Lines* represents Ila as bearing most heavily the burden of other people's expectations, and her unhappiness as the product of deep cultural contradictions" (Suvir Kaul: 131). She is surely the most deracinated character in the novel. One must therefore ask how this may also be true of the young narrator as he endeavours to recapture his childhood. Perhaps one would not be wrong to read the novel as the production of a talisman that may ward off Ila's "homeless" state.

Could it be that grandmother's accusations against Ila hang in the air as recurring accusations brought against any Indian in self-imposed exile? She apparently feels no pity for Ila, and declares that she has no right to live in England because the citizens of that nation have given their blood to define themselves, and Ila is a mere interloper. We are struck, in fact, by grandmother's harsh tone and her almost bloodthirsty dreams for her offspring. The narrator remembers his grandmother as someone bigger than life, a bubbling cauldron of nationalist fervor:

> [The English] know they're a nation because they've drawn their borders with blood. . . . That's what it takes to make a country. Once that happens people forget they were born this or that, Muslim or Hindu, Bengali or Punjabi: they become a family born of the same pool of blood. That is what *you* have to achieve for India, don't you see? (76)

Such nationalism is surely not valorised in Ghosh's writing, but grandmother has ironically identified its factitious commonality. It is surprising to hear such realpolitik coming from the mouth of a little old lady, until we later learn of the revolutionary nationalistic impulse in her youth. The narrator's insight into his grandmother, however stern and rigid her dismissal of Ila, is an all-embracing (metaphorical) hug: "All she wanted," he explains to the reader,

> was a middle-class life in which, like the middle classes the world over, she would thrive believing in the unity of nationhood and territory, of self-respect and national power; that was all she wanted – a modern, middle-class life, a small thing, that history had denied her in its fullness and for which she could never forgive it. (77)

And which of us, he seems to imply, would want anything less than she did? In effect, she becomes more than a little old lady in this novel, given the book's violent climax and given the narrator's struggle to make sense of emotional memories rooted in civil conflict. Grandmother was brought up on stories of Khudiram Bose and Bagha Jatin. She is, as Suvir Kaul puts it, "the exemplar of militant nationalism . . . who has lived the nationalist dream and experienced the set-backs and successes that give it its character" (135).

Thus, by contrasting Ila and grandmother, the narrator learns to distrust the dreams and ideals through which one interprets the raw data of daily experience. He realises, for example, that world-weary Ila has actually fabricated boyfriends in her various International Schools, and he says to himself: "I felt a constriction in my throat, for suddenly it seemed to me that perhaps she was not so alien, after all, to my own small, puritanical world, in which children were sent to school to learn how to cling to their gentility by proving themselves in the examination hall"

(23). What else, one might wonder, is one "sent to school" to learn? How malleable is the young child? In his own case, he has been taught to work hard and to accommodate himself to much that had been imposed by Britain. His grandmother had somehow been taught an enduring bloodlust. He is no longer taken in by Ila's dismissive façade that would have him believe she did not take life's struggles seriously. She no doubt understood grandmother long before the narrator did, and was in fact fleeing the world that was offered to her in India.

As a boy, the narrator listened closely and with wide eyes as grandmother told him about a young man about whom she sometimes still dreamed. He had been in class with her, long, long ago, and had been arrested for plotting to assassinate a British official. When the narrator asks her if she would have been willing to kill like that, he is astonished when she replies: "I would have been frightened, she said. But I would have prayed for strength, and God willing, yes, I would have killed him. It was for our freedom: I would have done anything to be free" (39). His reaction: "I gazed in awed disbelief at the delicate outline of her face, at the polished silver of her hair, and the filigreed tracery of veins on her cheek." His grandmother, on the other hand, "sat perched on the edge of her chair. . . , as fragile as a porcelain bird, smiling at the growing astonishment on my face as I tried to fit her into that extraordinary history" (37). There is something about the old lady's will that one cannot help but admire, but that smile is rather terrifying.

Ila is another story. The narrator has loved her all his life, but she never really loves him. Only gradually does he recognise how self-absorbed she is. Before the narrator comes to this realisation, Nick represents for him a rival for Ila's affections. He looms as a much larger symbol though, standing in for the British and all their impossible demands that people like the narrator change their spots and become something they are not:

> Nick Price... became a spectral presence beside me in my looking glass; growing with me, but always bigger and better, and in some ways more desirable.... And yet if I tried to look into the face of that ghostly presence, to see its nose, its teeth, its ears, there was never anything there, it had no features, no form; I would shut my eyes and try to see its face, but all I would see was a shock of yellow hair tumbling over a pair of bright blue eyes. (49)

When he meets Nick, though, he thinks he has found "at last the kindred spirit whom [he] had never been able to discover among [his] friends" (52). He has been taken in, in much the same way that Ila had been – both of them colonised by this pretty philanderer.

Ila and grandmother are set before the narrator as two magnetic poles tugging at his ego, forcing him to choose between them. In what must be seen as a mark of the narrator's growing maturity, he stays the course and finds his own path *between* the two. He chooses complexity – some would say, hybridity:

> I thought of how much they all [Ila, grandmother, and others like them] wanted to be free; how they went mad wanting their freedom; I began to wonder whether it was I that was mad because I was happy to be bound: whether I was alone in knowing that I could not live without the clamour of the voices within me. (88)

He will not choose the nationalistic bloodsport of his grandmother, nor the life outside time and space that seems Ila's fate. In a word, he identifies with his uncle

Tridib's choice. The narrator chooses this clamour of voices in full knowledge of its dangers – never finally settling one's identity, always teetering on the edge of nostalgia. His visit with his grandmother to their poor relation had taught him the wisdom of his father's injunction to work hard, because the wolf was at the door: In fact, if Nick Price had become all brightness and unattainable "Englishness" in his imagination, his poor relations had become the opposite pillar in that imagined world:

> I knew perfectly well that all it would take was a couple of failed examinations to put me where our relative was, in permanent proximity to that blackness: that landscape was the quicksand that seethed beneath the polished floors of our house; it was that sludge which gave our genteel decorum its fine edge of frenzy. (132)

Thus, he does not choose "freedom" in its conventional sense – the freedom of his grandmother's free nation, the freedom of Ila's nationless state – but instead chooses the freedom of the imagination, a freedom that looks with ever-renewed clarity at any false stasis.

The narrator recognises the journey that has brought him to this choice, and seeks to record its path. "I was determined now," he writes, "that I would not let my past vanish without a trace; I was determined to persuade [others] of its importance" (217). In his excellent study of several of Ghosh's works, Robert Dixon notes that *The Shadow Lines* is

> . . .a fictional critique of classical anthropology's model of discrete cultures and the associated ideology of nationalism. The 'reality' is the complex web of relationships between people that cut across nations and across generations . . .
> [so that]

> The Shadow Lines builds its critique of cultural borders upon the notion of a universal humanity. (Dixon:7)

R. K. Dhawan describes the book as a novel that resists classification:

> It is basically a memory novel that weaves together past and present, childhood and adulthood, India and Bangladesh and Britain, Hindu and Muslim. It is a social document and a political novel, a Bildungsroman and a postmodernist work of fiction. (Dhawan, 1999: 23)

In our discussion of *The Circle of Reason* and *The Shadow Lines* we have seen that the first is a story of flight and pursuit, very much an adventure story that involves elements of magic realism and seems consciously to imitate Salman Rushdie. The second marks a notable shift to a more strictly realistic examination of the protagonist's search through his memories, ultimately provoking a recognition in him and in the reader that he *too* was fleeing and pursuing something: namely, the connection between past and present in his own identity.

4. THE EBB AND FLOW OF PEOPLES ACROSS CONTINENTS AND GENERATIONS

IN AN ANTIQUE LAND, THE GLASS PALACE, THE HUNGRY TIDE

In An Antique Land

> It seemed uncanny that I had never known all those years that in defiance of the enforcers of History, a small remnant of Bomma's world had survived, not far from where I had been living. (*In An Antique Land*: 342)

The Story

Ghosh begins his account in Lataifa, the little Egyptian village where he stationed himself as an Oxford University graduate student in anthropology. Doctor Aly Issa, a professor at the University of Alexandria, has brought Ghosh to the home of Abu-'Ali, and it is there that he rents a room during his stay in Egypt. Ghosh does not especially relish living there, since Abu-'Ali, in his mid-fifties, is a somewhat overbearing small-businessman. In fact, Ghosh describes him as "profoundly unlovable" (23), but recognises him as someone who prompts a rather fearful respect from the villagers. After a while, Dr. Issa arranges for Ghosh to move out of Lataifa to Nashawy, a larger town.

Another of the major players in the village is Shaikh Musa, also in his mid-fifties, who runs a government-subsidised shop for retailing essential commodities at controlled prices. Ahmed and Jabir are his sons; Sakkina, their age, is Shaikh Musa's second wife (as Ghosh awkwardly discovers). She is the daughter of Ustaz ("teacher") Mustapha, and is Abu-'Ali's great grand-niece. The names begin to proliferate, and the reader begins to experience the disorientation that must have been Ghosh's, as well. As things develop, Mustapha – and a good many other people – seems to be interested in converting Ghosh to Islam. Most of the people that he meets, in fact, have at least a mild interest in welcoming him into their religious fold.

Ghosh left Egypt in 1981, and it was not for another seven years that he could again turn his attention with any seriousness to investigating Abraham Ben Yiju and his slave. He had learned some Arabic to communicate with his hosts, but that would not have been very helpful in his investigations. He had also spent time learning Judaeo-Arabic, a colloquial dialect of medieval Arabic written in Hebrew script that Ben Yiju had used. To his surprise and relief, he found that the dialect spoken in Lataifa and Nashawy in the twentieth century were not that remote from the "sounds" he was reading on Ben Yiju's pages. He learns that Ben Yiju had apparently lived in a Roman fortress nicknamed "Babylon" situated in the southern section of Cairo referred to as Old Cairo or Masr, called by some "the mother of the world" (80). It is also known as Masr al-Qadima, Masr al-'Atiqa, Mari Gargis, Fustat Masr, and Fustat – the inclusion of such arcane details shows Ghosh the student-researcher hard at work, but readers may sometimes wonder why he insists on giving us this forgotten set of titles. We remain patient, though, and read on, trusting that he knows what he is doing. Fustat served as Egypt's capital for more than three centuries. Cairo took its place, and Fustat today is attached to the metropolis as an immense rubbish-dump. The Ottoman Empire had reduced it in importance, and then the Indian Ocean trade that had made Fustat significant was supplanted in the eighteenth and nineteenth centuries by European navies.

The synagogue to which Ben Yiju belonged, (remember that he was Jewish), was made up of some very cosmopolitan individuals who had close ties with the Indian trade. Here is where the story begins to sound a bit like an Umberto Eco novel. This "Ben Ezra" congregation had a storehouse, as was customary, called a "geniza," in which all sorts of documents were stored. By a strange set of circumstances, the contents of this particular geniza were left undisturbed for more than seven hundred years, so that, upon its discovery, it was described as being "the greatest single collection of medieval documents ever discovered" (59). In the late 1600s, a fever of Egyptomania swept across Europe, but it was not until the mid-eighteenth century that the first report of the Ben Ezra geniza was published in Europe. Surprisingly, it was not until the *next* century that a scholarly visit to the geniza brought it significant attention. "By this time," writes Ghosh, "the indigenous Jews of Cairo, those whose relationship with the Synagogue of Ben Ezra was most direct, were a small and impoverished minority within the community" (85).

Ghosh traces the history of the various scholars, some obscure, who only very gradually succeeded in bringing the world's attention to the vast intellectual treasures that were secretly held in this out-of-the-way storeroom: Simon van Geldern, Jacob Saphir, Abraham Firkowitch, Paul Kahle, Elkan N. Adler, the Cattoui family, Solomon Schechter, Solomon Wertheimer, Agnes S. Lewis and Margaret D. Gibson, Charles Taylor, and others. The string that ties one to the next is tenuous but fascinating, and we also hear the wonder in Ghosh's voice – the voice of an academic researcher – that is excited by the facticity of historical materials: "By an extraordinary coincidence," he writes,

> it so happens that [a particularly significant] letter has survived and is currently lodged . . . in the library of the University of Cambridge. It is written on a fragment of paper of good, if not the best, quality, more than a foot in length, and about four inches wide. The paper is considerably weathered and discoloured; it is torn at the top, and there is a small hole in it that looks as though it has been caused by a burn. But the writing, which extends all the way down both sides, is clear and can be read without difficulty. (177-78)

Meanwhile, while studying these documents and following their lead back into the ins-and-outs of Ben Yiju's travels, Ghosh was also reacquainting himself with Shaikh Musa and the others who had befriended him on his first visit. He notices that there are now many more Egyptians working outside their country, principally in Iraq. In fact, of his younger friends from Lataifa, only Jabir has remained in Egypt. He also makes new acquaintances, and the narrator expands the list of names that he asks readers to learn. Among the most important is Imam

Ibrahim, who belonged to one of the two founding families of Nashawy. The other locally important family is the Badawy, far wealthier than the other group. In the course of his historical research, Ghosh also meets Ustaz Sabry, a young teacher who is writing a thesis on medieval Egyptian history. Two of Sabry's students, Nabeel and Ismail, are cousins. Ali, Nabeel's older brother, had worked in the fields to raise enough money to send Nabeel to school. Later, however, he makes a great deal of money overseas and is thereby enabled to marry Ismail's sister, Fawzia. In another family Ghosh makes friends with Khamees, Eid, and Busaina; these three pool all their resources at just the right moment and purchase land they had been working on as tenant farmers. In just a few years, they became among the wealthiest landowners in the village. Eid, in fact, manages to marry into the wealthy Badawy clan.

Ghosh continues his research and learns that Ben Yiju's father had been a rabbi. Two of his brothers, Yusuf and Mubashshir, are also mentioned in correspondence, as is a sister, Berakha. His mentor in business was the Chief Representative of merchants in Aden, Madmun ibn al-Hasan ibn Bundar. Without a definitive explanation available to him, Ghosh records that Ben Yiju apparently moved from Aden to the Malabar coast sometime before 1132, and did not return for nearly two decades. Ghosh surmises that he had left in order to escape some sort of blood feud. According to the Moroccan traveller Ibn Battuta, who visited Mangalore some two hundred years after Ben Yiju, the expatriate community of merchants from northern Africa and the Middle East lived very sumptuously. Ben Yiju likely associated more easily with the Muslim traders who were fellow expatriates in

Mangalore, and they all probably used a pidgin language to conduct business with the locals. Soon after his arrival in Mangalore, he frees a slave-girl named Ashu, and they marry. Ghosh notes that India, at the time, had a reputation as a place "notable for the ease of its sexual relations" (228). He speculates that Ben Yiju may have converted her to Judaism before the marriage, or that they had entered into "a kind of marital union that was widely practised by expatriate Iranian traders" – that is, the "temporary marriage" (230).

Ghosh also learns that, from 1143 onwards, Ben Yiju's homeland of Ifriqiya had come under successive attacks from Christians, and was ravaged by disease and famine. Most of his family, in fact, had relocated to Sicily without his knowledge. In 1149, he finally makes the trip back to Aden, now accompanied by his two adolescent children Surur (a son, who dies) and Sitt al-Dar (a daughter, who marries her cousin in Sicily in 1156). Three years after his arrival in Aden, he had apparently moved to Egypt, and at that point disappears from further historical records.

Ghosh travels to Mangalore in the summer of 1990 to see if he can learn any more about the slave mentioned in several of the Ben Yiju letters. He speaks with Professor Viveka Rai, an expert on the folklore of the area, and with a Jesuit priest named Father D'Souza. By a circuitous route, he concludes that the slave's name was probably Bomma and that he "had been born into one of the several matrilineal communities which played a part in the Bhuta-cult of Tulunad" (254). He further concludes that the relationship between Ben Yiju and Bomma was

> ...probably more that of patron and client than master and slave.... [because] in the Middle East and northern India.

> . . slavery was the principal means of recruitment into some of the most privileged sectors of the army and the bureaucracy. For those who made their way up through that route, 'slavery' was thus often a kind of career opening, a way of gaining entry into the highest levels of government. (259-60)

True to form, therefore, it seems that Bomma eventually assumed control of Ben Yiju's business interests in Aden, and that he assumed the title "Shaikh."

Themes and Concerns

In An Antique Land is an unusually constructed book that deals with themes of historical and cultural displacement, alienation, something we might call "subaltern cosmopolitanism," and the complexities of imagining another person's view of reality. The book is not recognisable as a novel, nor is it simply an historical investigation: it is a new genre, something that blends an anthropological record with a travelogue, a diary, and perhaps some imagined sections. The effect that this has on the reader is to force us to question whether particular events and characters are literally factual. "Within the parameters of history," Ghosh told one interviewer, "I have tried to capture a story, a narrative, without attempting to write a historical novel. You may say, as a writer, I have ventured on a technical innovation" (Dhawan, 1999: 24). Further complicating the categorisation is the fact that the narrative is set in two time periods: the first is roughly the present, and the second is the twelfth century. The book is based on the investigative work Amitav Ghosh conducted during his studies at Oxford University, in the course of which he lived in northern Egypt and tracked down the history of Abraham Ben Yiju, a mid-tweleth-century trader, and his slave, to whom a few letters from the time refer. The first of these letters was written in 1148 in Aden, by one Khalaf ibn Ishaq. It is addressed to Ben Yiju in Mangalore in south-western India. 1148 was the same year that a large Crusader army had assembled outside Damascus, so this was a time of heightened political tensions. The letter came to scholarly attention in 1942, when E. Strauss wrote about it. The slave is next mentioned in another of Khalaf ibn Ishaq's Aden letters, actually a letter written nine years earlier but not written *about* until thirty-one years after Strauss's first article. In both articles, there seems little concern about the serious political conflicts of the age, and all attention is instead focused on commerce. Ben Yiju is a Jewish merchant from Tunisia who had become wealthy through commerce with India, and who had died in Egypt. His various papers were discovered centuries later in a synagogue in Cairo. His slave is simply described in the letter as Ben Yiju's Indian "slave and business agent, a respected member of his household" (18).

As happens with many graduate students who are hunting for a topic for their thesis or dissertation, Ghosh chanced upon these letters in a library at Oxford in 1978 when he was working on social anthropology. As he describes them, they are "tiny threads, woven into the borders of a gigantic tapestry" (95). We have here the first suggestion of the theme of *In An Antique Land*: a demonstration of the manner in which the strands of the past connect to the present day. The threads become all-consuming to the graduate student, though, offering themselves as a possible

Rosetta Stone that will be a key to the unravelling of the "weave" of a particular culture. Before he knew it, Ghosh had left the ivied walls of Oxford and was off to Tunisia learning Arabic. Then he was off to Lataifa, an Egyptian village a couple of hours south-east of Alexandria – little knowing at the time that this book, published some twelve years later, was in the making.

Those who have undertaken a similar academic "journey" will quickly identify with the structure of this book, which begins with the actual journey to Egypt and an account of the author's response to his immediate surroundings, and then soon plunges into libraries, books, documents, and the imagined voyage back in time to the interlocking worlds of twelfth-century trade between Egypt and India. Much information in the final book has to be speculation that raises as many questions as it answers. Ghosh's conclusions, like those of any researcher into antiquities, remain tentative, but unlike many such researchers his conclusions are richly imagined and engagingly described. One understands how a graduate student might devote so much energy to two obscure individuals. In the course of human progress, after all, Ben Yiju and his slave are nobodies. Something about the process of their discovery, though, prompts Ghosh to bring his findings before a much larger audience than his dissertation committee.

This may involve the new sense of self that Ghosh develops as he experiences himself as an outsider. Like most immigrants he felt alienated when he arrived in Britain for his studies, but that was nothing compared to the alienation that besets him in the Egyptian village of Nashawy. At one point, for example, Abu-'Ali offers him some money to tide him over, but Ghosh is suspicious of the motivations:

> I stared at the wallet, mesmerised, wondering whether custom demanded that I touch it or make some other symbolic gesture of acceptance or obeisance, like falling at his feet. I saw myself shrinking, dwindling away into one of those tiny, terrified foreigners whom Pharaohs hold up by their hair in New Kingdom bas-reliefs. (30)

He imagines himself from outside and sees himself "shrinking, dwindling away," and this certainly rings true for anyone who is travelling in another country and has to negotiate another language and set of customs: it can be infantilising. That may explain his further statement, in which he projects onto his hosts the image of a mean-spirited Pharaoh. Ghosh the student, in other words, seems as capable of orientalising tendencies as any Western tourist might be, finding the occasion to enact his learned images of ancient times in his encounters with present-day Egyptians. In such a projected scenario, the people of Nashawy are not simply insensitive to his different customs: they are exotic torturers who represent an odd and fascist (and, as it happens, Muslim) regime. In such circumstances, he experiences himself as someone almost without a voice, someone who cannot adequately represent himself in the greater society of the powerful "Pharaohs."

In Nashawy, Ghosh had "soon discovered that salaried people like [Mustapha], rural mowazzafeen, were almost without exception absorbed in a concern which, despite its plural appearance, was actually single and indivisible – religion and politics – so that the mention of the one always led to the other" (50). At one point Mustapha goes so far as to apologise for some of his relatives who were working in a vegetable patch: "'They are fellaheen,' he said apologetically. 'They don't have much interest in religion or anything important'" (51). Ghosh concludes that there is a kind of caste system in this regard: based upon Mustapha's comments, at any rate, the poor are less interested in blending religion and politics than are the bourgeoisie Muslims. Thus, the anthropologist in Ghosh begins to distinguish between the interests of upper and lower castes in the Egyptian community – and seems to align himself with the lower caste that does not seek to oppress him with their religious beliefs.

As a "non-Muslim" he becomes increasingly aware of and uncomfortable about the "exclusion" he feels. This is, of course, especially the case during Ramadan, when he is not called upon to fast as are the others around him. He realises that Muslims all over the world are undergoing the same ritual, and he is struck by the attraction of that global community. "A phenomenon on that scale was beyond my imagining," he admits, "but the exercise helped me understand why so many people in the hamlet had told me not to fast: to belong to that immense community was a privilege they had to re-earn every year, and the effort made them doubly conscious of the value of its boundaries" (76).

On his return visit to Nashawy in 1988, Ghosh is again struck by the sense of exclusion that quickly overtakes him, prompted by questions about the customs of Indians: did they bury their dead, or cremate them? Was he circumcised? Did they worship cows? Is there military service for all in India, as there is in Egypt? How can you not purify [i.e., infibulate, or circumcise] your women? He tries his best to patiently answer the repeated questions. Typical of the responses to his answers is that from one female acquaintance, who tells him "You must put an end to this burning business... When you go back you should tell them about our ways and how we do these things" (169). He becomes increasingly upset over the repeated onslaught of the same series of questions, and confides to the reader a personal memory that he wishes he had shared with his Egyptian friends. It was as follows: when Ghosh was six years old, his father was working in the Indian diplomatic mission in East Pakistan. His ancestral roots, in fact, were in this region, but recent ancestors had migrated westward and the Ghosh family now identified themselves as Indians. As time went by, he noticed there were occasionally groups of Indians that would gather within the high-walled compound of his family's home, and it was not until later that he recognised that they were refugees fleeing from mobs. On one particular day in January of 1964 – that momentous year – his father told him to stay upstairs with their cook, with the shutters closed and the door firmly shut. All day long the garden had been filling with people. The cook was visibly frightened. Young Ghosh could see, beyond the walls, a swelling mob:

> I can see the enraged mob and the dancing flames with a vivid, burning clarity, yet all of it happens in utter silence; my memory, in an act of benign protection, has excised every single sound. (208)

At one point, his father returns briefly and retrieves a revolver. Later, Ghosh learns that on this same night there had been riots in Calcutta, as well, but in that city the mob was made up of Hindus attacking Muslims. In both cities, there had been exceptional people who had hidden away some of those whom their compatriots were threatening, but the scene around his house left an indelible mark on young Ghosh's memory:

> The stories of those riots are always the same: tales that grow out of an explosive barrier of symbols – of cities going up in flames because of a cow found dead in a temple or a pig in a mosque; of people killed for wearing a lungi or a dhoti, depending on where they find themselves; of women disembowelled for wearing veils or vermilion, of men dismembered for the state of their foreskins. But I was never able to explain very much of this to Nabeel or anyone else in Nashawy . . . theirs was a world that was far gentler, far less violent, very much more humane and innocent than mine. I could not have expected them to understand an Indian's terror of symbols. (210)

He recounts this story for the reader's benefit, but does not share it with the questioning Egyptians. One can understand why he might wish to keep quiet about this experience, especially if he knows that his hosts already think poorly of Indians. But Gauri Visnawathan offers an intriguing interpretation of his silence:

> The interrogator is interrogated for the bizarre practices of his own culture, and the frustration of being unable to explain either himself or his culture causes the narrator to veer off into another project, another narrative, this time of a twelfth-century Jewish merchant and his Indian slave. Onto this tale is displaced the impossibility of the ethnographic pursuit: tracing the genealogy of an anonymous slave restores the familiarity of an historical quest in which questions about origins, development, history, purpose, and teleology can be safely asked without the embarrassing dialectical intrusiveness of counter-questions posed by the very people who are being studied by the anthropologist. (Viswanathan: 20-21)

He can, in effect, thereby guarantee that the subaltern cannot speak – cannot ask him more embarrassing questions about his *own* culture's oddities. Robert Dixon raises a point that parallels Viswanathan's concerns, but approaches it from the viewpoint of the ephemeral *object* of Ghosh's anthropological investigation:

> 'Bomma' is the subaltern consciousness," writes Dixon, "whose recovery justifies Ghosh's allegorical reading of the destruction of a polyglot trading culture by Western influence. Unlike some contributors to *Subaltern Studies*, Ghosh develops a style of writing that is sufficiently nuanced and elusive to sustain the 'theoretical fiction' of a recovery of presence without actually falling back into essentialism. (Robert Dixon, 1996: 18)

Thus, since Bomma remains really very elusive and finally a pretty speculative figure, Ghosh can limit his outlines without over-interpreting his "content." He is not only a subaltern who cannot speak, but also one that Ghosh uncovers/discovers and thereby owns. This provides, perhaps, a certain amount of comfort when one is surrounded by hostile Pharaohs! Notice, as well, the proliferation of names in the contemporary sections of the book. This is quite disorienting, as if one is beset by a mass of indistinguishable otherness, whereas the work in the library is a welcome bit of controlled narration. One can only surmise that this echoes Ghosh's own experiences.

The fate of the many historically invaluable documents in the Ben Ezra synagogue's Geniza, drawing Ghosh's attention so early in his creative life, possibly underscores the source of a theme that follows through in most of his writing: the different windows that we each have on the world around us, and on all that has come before us. What does one culture come to value, and another choose to ignore or denigrate? What are the philosophical implications of viewing the world through the eyes of an Indian, as opposed to a Russian or a Kenyan? In *The Circle of Reason*, Balaram becomes obsessed with phrenology and with carbolic acid; Toru-debi defines herself in terms of her sewing machine; Jyoti Das lives to pursue the "criminal" Alu. In *The Shadow Lines*, the narrator reads the rest of his life through the single experience of his uncle's murder. In *The Hungry Tide*, Piya lives for the dolphins she studies; Kanai finds meaning in translation. In *The Calcutta Chromosome*, one character is a fanatic researcher into the life of a Victorian biologist. *In An Antique Land*, of course, documents Ghosh's own "obsession" with a very, very obscure slave from hundreds of years ago. Why do humans make these choices of the lens through which they view the rest of reality? And with what effect on their relations with others in the world?

But in the gradual removal of the properties to Europe, Ghosh also sees a symbol of the actions of colonisers everywhere, whether for commercial, religious, or intellectual purposes: "a view of the world in which the interests of the powerful defined necessity, while the demands of the poor appeared as greed" (94). Thus, Ghosh notes that

> ... by the First World War, the Geniza had finally been emptied of all its documents. In its home country however, nobody took the slightest notice of its dispersal. In some profound sense, the Islamic high culture of Masr had never really noticed, never found a place for the parallel history the Geniza represented [that is, the Jewish history], and its removal only confirmed a particular vision of the past... It was as though the borders that were to divide Palestine several decades later had already been drawn, through time rather than territory, to allocate a choice of Histories. (95)

The phrase is very meaningful: a choice of histories, suggesting that what we choose to focus on as "history" will very much shape how we subsequently determine who counts as historically significant. In this case, it was to be the Muslim version that counted, so the Geniza documents (Jewish) might just as well be carted off to Europe and, from an Islamic point of view, fall into oblivion once more.

Getting to speak with Imam Ibrahim proves to be difficult, and carrying on a conversation with the crusty fellow is nearly impossible. But in the course of their awkward and prickly discussion, Ghosh makes an emotional discovery that is destined to influence all his future writing. He sees the two of them as "delegates from two superseded civilisations" who were suspiciously eyeing each other, sizing each other up, defining each other in terms mandated by the West:

> ... the Imam and I had participated in our own final defeat, in the dissolution of the centuries of dialogue that had linked us: we had demonstrated the irreversible triumph of the language that has usurped all the others in which people once discussed their differences. We had acknowledged that it was no longer possible to speak, as Ben Yiju or his Slave, or any one of the thousands of travellers who had crossed the Indian Ocean in the Middle Ages might have done ... for they belonged to a dismantled rung on the ascending ladder of Development. (236-37)

It seems to have been a crushing epiphany for the young scholar, almost eviscerating the rationale for his Oxonian studies. "I felt myself a conspirator in the betrayal of the history that had led me to Nashawy," he writes, "a witness to the extermination of a world of accommodations that I had believed to be still alive, and, in some tiny measure, still retrievable" (237). "Retrievable" seems to be a significant word here, forcing us to ask what the young (romantic?) anthropologist thought he was undertaking in heading off first to Oxford, then northern Africa. Reading his account, one cannot help but wonder if a stark confrontation with his own position as a cosmopolitan "Third Worlder" didn't trigger a reordering of the young graduate student's sense of his vocation – from recovery (history and anthropology) to creation (fiction writing). But, if so, such a *metanoia* (that is, a life-altering change of heart) would be a long time in unfolding its implications.

Among many of the Egyptians whom Ghosh met, there was a long tradition of members of the family travelling "outside" and making money for the family. He was struck that they almost uniformly found this a marvellous adventure: "for them the world outside was still replete with the wonders of the unknown. That was why our friendship was so quickly sealed" (174). But the longer he stays, the more eccentric he is made to feel. They ask about India, but cannot be made to believe that there are actually poor people there. Finally, he comes to a striking insight not only into the people of Nashawy, but perhaps into all the "subaltern" classes in the world, and it is an insight that wars against his instincts as a novelist. He recognises that, for the poor of the world,

> ... mud-walled houses and cattle-drawn ploughs... were insubstantial things, ghosts displaced in time, waiting to be exercised and laid to rest. It was thus that I had my first suspicion of what it might mean to belong to an 'historical civilisation,' and it left me bewildered because, for my own part, it was precisely the absoluteness of time and the discreteness of epochs that I always had trouble in imagining. (200-201)

Again, much like Tridib in *The Shadow Lines*, Ghosh the graduate anthropology student seems to yearn for a type of syncretism – if not of religions, then of epochs. But what can that mean to him, one must wonder. Surely his writing *tries* to read the past in the present – he does have this palimpsestic imagination – but can this be meant literally? If the fellaheen are globalised enough to know of richer lives lived elsewhere, they surely cannot be said to be actually living in the past, can they? Samir Dayal very much appreciates what Ghosh is trying to do, writing that "the author, presenting himself as a traveller in the intercultural border zones, interstitially between the West and the non-West but also in-between modernity and other times, compels us to rethink diaspora, cultural mixture or cultural intercourse, and indeed 'hybridity' itself – which is a key concept in this volume" (131). But Gauri Viswanathan asks a more pointed question, having to do with the practical implications of the type of syncretism that Ghosh may be advocating in *In An Antique Land*: "no matter how moving Ghosh's book might be," writes Viswanathan, "and no matter how appealing his humanist call for dissolving barriers between nations, peoples, and communities on the grounds that world civilisations were syncretic long before the divisions introduced by the territorial boundaries of nation-states, the work cannot get beyond nostalgia to offer ways of dealing with what is, after all, an intractable political problem" (32). Ghosh is not writing a political treatise here, and really cannot be expected to set out an agenda for correcting a problem that he accurately observes. The question Viswanathan asks, though, is one worth pondering: "can syncretism issuing as a fiction of the state (and, by extension, also of dominant, elite groups) bear the burden of people's perceptions of themselves?" (33).

While in Mangalore, Ghosh learns a good deal about the history of the mercantile trade in the Indian Ocean before the Europeans arrived, and he finds that it had apparently been remarkably peaceful (except for the occasional assault by pirates). But in 1509, the Portuguese changed all that. Ghosh concludes: "soon, the remains of the civilisation that had brought Ben Yiju to Mangalore were devoured by that unquenchable, demonic thirst that has raged ever since, for almost five hundred years, over the Indian Ocean, the Arabian Sea and the Persian Gulf" (288). The message seems clear: India and Africa did very well with each other, living and trading peacefully for centuries, before the European coloniser intervened with violence. As a cosmopolitan Indian studying at Oxford, he must have experienced a certain sense of agency and control over his life, but after his studies and his conversation with Imam Ibrahim and others, he appears to have identified more closely with the "delegates of two superseded civilisations." In a sense, he has come to identify himself in this broader historic and geographic context as a member of this vast "subaltern" class.

Critical response to this unusual book has been generally positive, though probing questions have been raised by some readers. On the one hand, as we have seen, Gauri Viswanathan can read it in a negative manner, suggesting that

> ...the mercurial connotations of syncretism encode a set of relativised, partial, and often conflicting perspectives: what Hindus would call syncretic coexistence of religious faiths when they refer to "the Hindu way of life" might be termed "forced assimilation" by Muslims.... [Thus,] the use of the word syncretism effaces not only the aspect of domination but also the specific position from which

certain interests are advanced, presumably in the name of a larger comity of universal brotherhood. (31)

But others can read the same text and make a completely different judgement. Samir Dayal, for example, praises it as "a tale about the connections *among* non-Western cultures," that can leap over Eurocentric notions of identity; the book, in Dayal's words, is

> . . .a pretext for an approach to understanding subject formation in regions (specifically, Egypt and India) whose 'antique' cultures seem to disappear under the powerful spotlight of 'postcolonial' and even 'colonial' studies, as if these ancient cultures began to have an ontology only when Europeans 'discovered' them. (104)

But this does bring us back to the genre question. Here we have an Oxford-trained anthropologist writing about two individuals who lived hundreds of years ago, and about whom there is little public record. Why does he do so and, having made the decision, *how* can he do so? We have reason to believe, I think, that Ghosh has decided to read the present through the past, and vice versa – he comes to understand Bomma by coming to understand the people with whom he is living in Nashawy. Such a syncretic leap across centuries may be more than a little bit essentialist. But *how*, otherwise, is Bomma (or, for that matter, all the villagers of Nashawy) to speak to Ghosh's typical readers? Pointing to the author's strikingly *un*-scientific speculation about Ben Yiju's sexual interest in Ashu, and speculation of her possible conversion, etc., Samir Dayal notes that "this almost polemical and subversive unravelling of scientific methodology is one of the remarkable features of Ghosh's genre-bending text." Dayal goes so far as to suggest that it is this very inability of science to find a way for the subaltern to speak that has led Ghosh to give up anthropology in favour of fiction: "it is one of the reasons, one surmises, for Ghosh's having undertaken to construct such a hybrid artefact, suggesting that the author is somewhat disillusioned with the capacity of a scientifically pure social anthropology to capture the full-lived truth about the Slave" (Samir Dayal: 130). Perhaps in *In An Antique Land*, we are watching Amitav Ghosh make that decision, putting his Oxford degree to bed, and taking up the world of fiction-writing with full force. The subaltern *will* speak.

The Glass Palace

> Like many Indians I grew up on stories of other countries: places my parents and relatives had lived in or visited before the birth of the Republic of India in 1947. To me the most intriguing of these stories were those that my family carried out of Burma. (Afterword, *Burma: Something Went Wrong*. (Photos by Chan Chao))

> [I]n classical writing, everything happens outside ... But that is not how you write? 'No.' She laughed. ... nothing is more difficult for me than this – going into a house, intruding, violating. ... I feel a kind of terror – and that's when I know I must keep going, step in past the threshold, into the house. (*The Glass Palace*: 460)

The Story

The Glass Palace is rightly described by John Thieme as a family saga (Thieme: Ghosh), and it is quite lengthy and involved. It opens in Mandalay in 1885; eleven-year-old orphan Rajkumar finds himself stranded when the sampan on which he works as a serving-boy has to be put into port for repairs. He is from Chittagong, but his father had moved them to Akyab, an important Burmese port. En route, his family tragically dies of fever. His mother's dying words to him are: "Live, my Prince; hold on to your life" (12) – and that, in a nutshell, is exactly what he does, for good or ill.

In Mandalay, Rajkumar meets Ma Cho. She is half-Indian/half-Chinese, in her mid-thirties, and she runs a small food-stall. Ma Cho employs him as an errand boy. Time passes. She introduces him to her "teacher" and lover, Saya John Martins, who is a Chinese contractor who also happens to be a Christian. He is something like an older Rajkumar, since he also had been orphaned and thereafter became a world traveller. He learned a good many languages in the process, but doesn't "belong" anywhere. Saya John introduces Rajkumar to his seven-year-old son Matthew; he is visiting from Singapore, where he attends a well-known missionary school. Saya John decides to employ Rajkumar, and Rajkumar moves into his home. They begin trading in teak.

As it happens, Rajkumar has arrived in Mandalay just as the British are taking over the country. In the thirty-year-old "glass palace" live twenty-seven-year-old Thebaw (1885-1916), King of Burma, and Supayalat. She is his haughty and ruthless chief consort, and has had assassinated all family members who might challenge her husband's right to the throne – there were seventy-nine such claimants! Her closest maids are orphans, and Dolly is the youngest and most beautiful of them.

Supayalat is clearly the power behind the throne; the King, on the other hand, is kept in blissful ignorance by his advisors. In fact, he had not stepped out of the palace in seven years and had never left Mandalay! In just fourteen days, the British force the King to surrender. As the troops enter the city, Ma Cho and others enter the palace compound, which had until then been completely off limits to them – and ransack it. In the melee, Rajkumar encounters the maid, Dolly, and is so struck by her beauty that he puts back into her hands the jewelled ivory box he had intended to steal. Colonel Sladen escorts the royal family into exile – first to Madras, and then *more permanently* to Ratnagiri, hundred and twenty miles south of Bombay. They live in "Outram House," which is on a hill overlooking the town. A local man named Sawant takes charge of the servants. Time passes. Dolly loses her virginity to Sawant. When plague breaks out, the villagers move up to the King's compound for greater safety.

In 1905, an Indian named Beni Prasad-Dey arrives in Ratnagiri as the new District Collector. The Burmese royal family and the few retainers who have not deserted have now lived in the town for twenty years. Beni Prasad-Dey has been educated in England and is, in fact, one of the few Indians in the British civil service who has such a high office. His wife, Uma, is fifteen years his junior, and she lives somewhat in his shadow. Their house is known as the Residency. Uma quickly makes friends with Dolly, who has become a beautiful and gracious young woman. Uma at this time is twenty-six and has been married five years; Dolly is just a few years older than that. Uma begins worrying for her and for the princesses, as well, wondering whether they are ever going to be able to marry. That is soon answered, as the first princess is found to be pregnant by Sawant. To the annoyance of the British, but bitter delight of Supayalat, they marry and move away.

Meanwhile, in the inland Burmese town of Huay Zedi, situated on the Sittang River, Rajkumar makes friends with Doh Say. When they meet, Doh Say, a couple of years his senior, is an elephant herder working in the teak forests. Rajkumar determines to become wealthy, and hatches a scheme to make money by importing workers from India for British oil fields. With this money, and a bit from Saya John, he buys a large teak forest and, after a good number of years of hard work, establishes a profitable plantation. He becomes quite skilful at negotiation and lands a plum contract with the company that is building a new railroad into the various teak areas. Part of his success is aided by Uma's uncle, D. P. Roy, who is a banker in Rangoon. (Again, the number of characters in a Ghosh novel can be a bit daunting.) This serendipitous connection leads Rajkumar, who is now thirty and rich, to decide to visit Ratnagiri and look for Dolly: he has never forgotten her since their very brief encounter so many years before when the King was exiled. He is an odd combination, as may now be obvious, of romanticism and hard-headed business know-how. After much hesitation, Dolly is convinced that Rajkumar's love for her is genuine. The two are married in a small ceremony, presided over by Uma's husband. Supayalat, however, is infuriated: she had wanted Dolly to work for her forever, and she now refuses to see Dolly ever again.

As intermediary between the British and the Burmese royal family, Beni Prasad-Dey had been placed in a most awkward situation by the pregnancy of the princess and the prospect of her marriage to the Indian, Sawant. Perhaps because of the sheer number of characters in the novel, the reader has not been allowed to spend much time with Prasad. He comes across as a somewhat ineffectual and even comic pawn of the British. Now, however, he suddenly becomes something of a tragic hero. The news of his demotion has come at an especially bad time, since Uma had just decided to leave him and to return to her parents' home. Prasad cannot face this double reversal of his fortunes, and subsequently drowns himself in the sea. Since her husband had filled such a significant governmental position, Uma now received a substantial pension. She has freedom, and money. She books passage to Europe, and in London she becomes a leader of the movement to free India. She visits the United States and raises money for the cause, and settles in New York where Saya John's son, Matthew, was living. Matthew meanwhile marries an American named Elsa Hoffman. Uma later urges him to return to visit his rather estranged father, who increasingly is in need of his son's help.

Dolly and Rajkumar had initially moved in with Saya John in Rangoon. This was her first visit to Burma since she had left, twenty-five years before. Saya John and Rajkumar's latest commercial venture was the growing of rubber trees, and they had established a plantation on Penang island. Elsa and Matthew come to live there, as well, and Elsa gives it its name: Morningside Rubber Estate. Soon Dolly gives birth to her first son, Neeladhri (Neel), who seems increasingly to have many of Rajkumar's characteristics. Four years later, Dolly gives birth to her second son, Dinanath (Dinu), whose temperament seems a good bit like her own. Unfortunately, Dinu develops polio but is taken to the hospital in time to avoid serious after-effects. But because Dinu is frail, Dolly dotes too much on him. An odd thing had happened: the old Burmese king for whom young Dolly had worked had appeared to her in a dream, warning her that Dinu's fever was very significant, and the child had to go immediately to the hospital – and he had been correct: it was, in fact, polio. The next day, after having seen the doctor, Dolly learns that the king had died the very night that he had appeared to her in a dream. In fact, we learn that the king had died soon after the second princess had eloped with a commoner.

In 1929, Uma is fifty, and she writes to Dolly to tell her that she is leaving America and returning to Calcutta. Dinu is fourteen now; Neel is eighteen. Matthew and Elea had a daughter, Alison, and now also have a son, named Timmy. Dolly decides to take her two sons to Malaya and invites Uma to meet with them at the rubber plantation at Morningside House. It is twenty-three years since they last saw each other, and that was in Rangoon. In this span of time, Uma has transformed herself into a political force. So Uma does visit Dolly, but she soon angrily denounces Rajkumar as a British collaborator. After this clash, she leaves for Calcutta. Her brother meets her at the airport in Calcutta, along with his twin children, Arjun and Manju, and the youngest child, his daughter Bela. Surprisingly, in the new setting Uma's virulent political thinking soon changes drastically. As the Burmese rebellion fails, her thoughts turn to Gandhi's non-violent methods, and she volunteers her services to his cause.

If Uma has chosen the way of passive resistance, her nephew Arjun definitely has not. He enters the Indian Military Academy in Dehra Dun and happily finds an identity there. His sister Manju, on the other hand, hopes to become an actress. In a strange bit of serendipity, the producer of the film for which she had planned to audition turns out to be Neel, Dolly and Rajkumar's son. A romance blossoms between the two and they are soon married. Arjun, meanwhile, is delighted at what he perceives to be an egalitarian spirit in the army, and is complimented by the position of leadership in which he is placed. Arjun is one of the few Indians at the Academy, and he learns to take his lead from another Indian there named Hardayal, whose family had a tradition of military service with the British. Despite his family's long connection to the British military, however, Hardayal is growing increasingly restless in that role, increasingly sceptical of the use to which the British are putting Indians like himself.

The pace of events in the novel begins to accelerate. Back in Europe, Britain is declaring war on Germany. In Rajkumar's world, though, the focus is on his developing pneumonia. He interprets the enforced rest as an occasion to reassess his businesses and decides to sell his properties before things become dangerous in Burma. Ever the businessman, he decides to sell all his assets to finance the purchase of great quantities of timber: he is anticipating that the British and Dutch will need to reinforce their defences throughout the East. Dolly accuses him of war-profiteering. Alison meanwhile receives word that her parents, Matthew and Elsa, have died in a car crash in the Cameron Highlands. Arjun and his battalion, up to this time having little to do, are sent to the frontiers of Afghanistan. That is where he first hears of a Sikh unit having mutinied in Bombay. Arjun and Hardayal are both full lieutenants now and are among the few regular army officers left in their unit. Hardayal's doubts grow, and they begin to plague Arjun, as well.

Dinu, now twenty-seven and very interested in photography, arrives at Morningside House and strikes up a friendship with Alison. With the death of her parents, she finds that the boundaries that shored up her identity have come loose. During his visit, Dinu falls in love with Alison. Just as momentously, he learns that the servant Ilongo is his half-brother.

Soon Arjun's battalion is on its way to Singapore. They work their way up the Malay peninsula as rumours of a Japanese air attack begin circulating. Soon, various units begin deserting. Arjun is wounded and has to hide from the invading Japanese in a storm-drain with his batman, Kishan Singh. Singh's comparatively lesser prospects in life had prompted Arjun to muse about his own place in history. The next morning they emerge from the storm-drain and are happy to find Hardayal, but he has by now allied himself with the Indian national movement, whose members have gone over to the Japanese side – at least for the time being. This is the last straw for Arjun, who despairs of his former course and decides to follow Hardayal's lead.

With the Japanese on their way, Alison, Dinu, Saya John, and Ilongo make plans to leave for Singapore, but when they reach the railway station they are horrified to learn that only Europeans would be allowed in the trains. The encounter brings Dinu to a kind of political consciousness (as his time in the trenches had done for Arjun), and he fights with the Indian officials who are enforcing the British rules by keeping the non-Europeans off the train. In desperation they head back to the plantation. Dinu encourages Alison to leave by car with Saya John, who is, of course, quite elderly by now, and Dinu promises he will try to join them in Singapore. They drive off and travel as far as they can before they decide to catch a bit of sleep. When Alison wakes up in the morning, though, she becomes very distressed in seeing that Saya John has

The Ebb and Flow of Peoples... 111

wandered away. She looks down the road and sees that he is being questioned up ahead by Japanese soldiers. She fires in their direction. Instead of scaring them off, however, her actions prompt them to shoot Saya John immediately and then to head in her direction. As they approach her, she shoots herself – she has followed Beni Prasad-Dey's sad path.

In Rangoon, meanwhile, Manju has given birth to Jaya, a little girl. It might be a cause for celebration, but there is little time for that: a representative of the Indian community arrives to warn them all to evacuate Burma that evening. Meanwhile, Neel has taken over management of his father's attempt to sell his properties and buy timber and has met with success – a victory that turns out to be pyrrhic: all Rajkumar's funds have been invested in one plantation, and when the Japanese *bomb* nearby, the elephants panic; Neel is crushed to death and the trees are destroyed in the melee. Rajkumar has lost everything – Neel and the money. Having waited too long, Manju, Dolly, Rajkumar and the baby now try to get away. They join some thirty thousand refugees who are trying to cross the river. In her own despair at the loss of Neel, Manju quietly slips beneath the surface and drowns herself – another member of the family lost to despair. She had recognised that Dolly and Rajkumar were a different breed of individuals – hungry for life – and she knew her baby would learn to grasp life far better from their ageing hands.

Dolly and Rajkumar stay with Uma in her flat for the next six years; then Dolly travels to Rangoon hoping to locate Dinu. Rajkumar never sees her again. In 1948, she finds Dinu, stays with him for a while, and then spends her last days in a nunnery. Time passes. Jaya marries young, at seventeen, a doctor ten years her senior.

In 1996, she is a college professor and her college sends her to an art history conference at the University of Goa. While there, she meets a "pioneering photographer from the early years of the century," and discovers that he is, in fact, her uncle Dinu. Though he is now eighty-two years old, she decides to visit him, and finds that he works in a studio he calls "The Glass Palace." The reader senses that we have somehow come full circle. Dinu also quietly conducts classes much like those of Aung San Suu Kyi. Like her, he had been imprisoned by the Burmese dictatorial military for three years. His classes focus on aesthetics, but they imply a philosophy with political ramifications.

Jaya learns that Dinu had left Malay shortly after Alison's death and had made his way to Rangoon in June of 1942. He had gone in search of Arjun, and finally found him – wasted away, wounded and dying. Dinu had gone on to marry Ma Thin Thin Aye, the young girl who had helped to shelter him when he had passed through Rangoon in 1942. The two of them came to a greater political consciousness from listening to the lectures given by Aung San Suu Kyi. Jaya tells Dinu that Rajkumar and Dolly, though far apart from each other, had both died within a few days of each other, both of them almost ninety.

Themes and Concerns

The first of the quotes serving as epigraph to our discussion of *The Glass Palace* refers to the content of this novel; the second refers to its technique. It seems a very different world, indeed, from the two described in *In An Antique Land*. Both, however, ponder the *effects of history on*

The Ebb and Flow of Peoples...   *113*

individual lives; both take special care to focus central attention on "minor" characters; both challenge the notion of boundaries and imperial definitions.

In discussing *In An Antique Land*'s history of the mercantile trade between India and Africa in medieval times, Samir Dayal had remarked that it showed that "cosmopolitanism is not to be claimed as exclusively the fruit of Western expansionism" (Dayal: 113), and this theme clearly continues into *The Glass Palace*.

Set principally in Burma and Malaya, *The Glass Palace* spans several generations and is partially based upon the experiences of Ghosh's uncle, Jagat Chandra Dutta, who had been a timber merchant in Burma. In his 17 July 2000 interview with *Outlook*, Ghosh mentioned that his father's family had lived in Burma for several generations. His motivation in writing such a novel, therefore, is first of all personal: it is an imaginative recollection of part of his family history – though we are left to imagine how much of the novel is factual. He feels a great attraction to the country. But he is disturbed by its recent history and describes it as essentially two countries. He had a great deal of trouble trying to evade constant surveillance as he tried to research for his novel

Part of his motivation, though, is to record a portion of history that might otherwise simply pass out of public record. Regarding the Long March, when Indians fled Burma fearing Japanese occupation, Ghosh told a reporter that

> . . . it's not been written about at all. . . . It's strange – there were over half a million people on the Long March, over 400,000 of them Indian, and there is such a silence about it. . . . There was no need for the Indians in Burma

to flee when the Japanese approached – many Indians did stay back. It makes you realise the degree to which Indians felt themselves to be the sheep of the British; the delusions that governed their lives. (*Outlook* interview, 17 July 2000)

The final comment suggests a corollary to this reason for writing the novel: he wishes, also, to underscore that British occupation was not an unmixed blessing. In a good many cases, it was not a blessing, at all. Early in the novel, Ghosh notes that "this is how power is eclipsed: in a moment of vivid realism, between the waning of one fantasy of governance and its replacement by the next; in an instant when the world springs free of its mooring of dreams and reveals itself to be girdled in the pathways of survival and self-preservation" (36). We see this played out in the individual histories of these interlocking families – some endure in the face of massive shifts in fate; others succumb. In his rejection of the nomination of this book for the Commonwealth Writers' Prize, Ghosh has written that "the issue of how the past is to be remembered lies at the heart of *The Glass Palace* and I feel that I would be betraying the spirit of my book if I were to allow it to be incorporated within that particular memorialisation of Empire that passes under the rubric of 'the Commonwealth'" (Ghosh, PEN 35-36). It is in the care with which he renders the lives of otherwise insignificant individuals that Ghosh shows what he means by "how" the past is to be remembered: not as an imperial chess game, but as biographies of otherwise unknown people. Who has the right to determine whose lives "count"? Thinking again of the Indian Rebellion of the mid-Victorian period, who is to say which of those involved is to be remembered as heroic, and who remembered as villainous? And of the many who were involved but never

The Ebb and Flow of Peoples...

remembered to this day – what does such historic neglect tell us of the arbitrary nature of *our* version of "history"?

In one of many postcolonial manoeuvres in this novel, Ghosh has the King ponder his fate and the fate of empires as he is on his way into exile. In Rangoon, where the British had transported almost more Indians than there were Burmese, the King pauses to think on his way to exile in India.

> The King raised his glasses to his eyes and spotted several Indian faces along the waterfront. What vast, what incomprehensible power, to move people in such numbers from one place to another – emperors, kings, farmers, dockworkers, soldiers, coolies, policemen. Why? Why this furious movement – people taken from one place to another, to pull rickshaws, to sit blind in exile? (43-44)

Of course, the fate of exiles of various sorts recurs in Ghosh's writing as an inscrutable problem in history.

When the British visit Outram House to investigate the princess's marriage to a commoner, Supayalat takes her narrative turn as the postcolonial critic:

> In a few decades the wealth will be gone – all the gems, the timber and the oil – and then they too will leave.... This is what awaits us all; this is how we will all end – as prisoners, in shantytowns born of the plague. A hundred years hence you will read the indictment of Europe's greed in the difference between the kingdom of Siam and the state of our own enslaved realm. (76)

The princess herself, of course, is no great friend to her country (she was notoriously cruel and, according to Kenneth Champeon, "only a smattering of Burmese nationalists saw her as a legitimate representative of her country"). But her prophecy has an angry ring to it, with an indictment that stretches beyond the confines of this novel.

And, though he works for the British and though he keeps his protest unspoken, Beni Prasad-Dey also recognises the racist framework that guides their policies in the colonies. As he puts it,

> ...the smell of miscegenation has alarmed [the British] as nothing else could have: they are tolerant in many things, but not this. They like to keep their races tidily separate. The prospect of dealing with a half-caste bastard has set them rampaging among their desks. (149)

As he predicts, they recall him in disgrace.

But if Uma followed her husband's lead and kept her silence while he worked for the British, after his death she definitely spoke her protest loudly and clearly. She was, after all, only twenty-eight when her husband committed suicide. She had lived in his shadow, but had developed strong opinions – of him, and of his role in the British empire. After Prasad's death she remembers him mostly as a mimic man, a lackey of the coloniser:

> There seemed never to be a moment when he was not haunted by the fear of being thought lacking by his British colleagues. And yet it seemed to be universally agreed that he was one of the most successful Indians of his generation, a model for his countrymen. Did this mean that one day all of India would become a shadow of what he had been? Millions of people trying to live their lives in conformity with incomprehensible rules? Better to be what Dolly had been: a woman who had no illusions about the nature of her condition; a prisoner who knew the exact dimensions of her cage and could look for contentment within those confines. (161-62)

One senses that Ghosh is using this character to challenge contemporary Indians who have a special relationship with Britain. V. S. Naipaul was one of the important novelists who inspired Ghosh to take up fiction writing, and one thinks here of his masterpiece, *The Mimic Men*, whose central character speaks of being a "prisoner of his role." "We learned about power," he writes. "We learned about our poverty. The two went together, but it was our poverty which made the understanding of power more urgent" (Naipaul: 244). Uma makes the challenge, but does not offer a clear response. In fact, in her own life it still takes her some time after her husband's death to find her new role in life. But when she awakens from these years of relative slumber, she becomes a revolutionary. Like her contemporary, Lala Hardayal, Uma recognises that "the conditions being created in their homeland were such as to ensure that their descendants would enter the new epoch as cripples," so that "they would truly become in the future what they had never been in the past, a burden upon the world." She therefore works to "change the angle of their country's entry into the future" (191-92).

Among the principal tasks she sets herself is "to open the soldiers' eyes" (193). She had heard from those who had gained a greater self of Indian national identity that the British had told their Indian sepoys that they were freeing people "from their bad kings or their evil customs or some such thing," and they had believed it because the British had believed it. "It took us a long time to understand," the soldier had told her, "that in their eyes freedom exists wherever *they* rule" (193). Such an insight has deep roots in the history of Britain and India. Thomas Babington Macaulay, for example, wrote in his "Introductory Report upon the Indian Penal Code" in 1837 that:

> It appears to us that none of the systems of penal law established in British India has any claim to our attention, except what it may derive from its own intrinsic excellence. All those systems are foreign. All were introduced by conquerors differing in race, manners, language, and religion from the great mass of the people. The criminal law of the Hindoos was long ago superseded, through the greater part of the territories now subject to the [British East India] Company, by that of the Mahometans, and is certainly the last system of criminal law which an enlightened and humane government would be disposed to revive. The Mahometan criminal law has in its turn been superseded, to a great extent, by the British Regulations. (Macaulay: 75)

In her proclamation of 1 November, 1858, Queen Victoria declared that "when, by the blessing of Providence, internal tranquillity shall be restored, it is our earnest desire to stimulate the peaceful industry of India, to promote works of public utility and improvement, and to administer its government for the benefit of all our subjects resident therein" (Victoria: 210). Twenty-six years later, the Ilbert Bill was passed and native Indians could be judges over resident Britons. This prompted a huge negative reaction from those Britons, expressed in an editorial in *The Times* of London on 26 February 1883:

> Those who stake their stand upon some abstract theory or sentiment may, of course, exclaim fiat justitia [let justice be done] after the magnificent manner of sentimentalists everywhere, but practical politicians will agree with us in thinking that the universal opinion of the European community cannot be thus lightly disposed of. We do not govern India exclusively through the Civil Service. Every man who plants tea or indigo or cinchona, who exports wheat, or who runs a mill, is part of an agency for the development of India which is the necessary complement of the machinery of government. (*The Times*: 220)

This Victorian policy plays itself out before Uma's eyes when Indians clash with Burmese who wish to separate Burma from British rule. She considers Rajkumar a neo-colonialist, and shouts at him:

> It's people like you who're responsible for this tragedy. Did you ever think of the consequences when you were transporting people here? What you and your kind have done is far worse than the worst deeds of the Europeans. (214)

Complicity in the colonising mission becomes the great evil that Uma sets herself against.

More pointedly, the ethics of serving in someone else's army is a theme that runs through the novel: Saya John inveighs against troops of the Indian sepoys (two-thirds of the ten thousand strong British force that displaced the Burmese King), whom he describes as "an enemy who fights from neither enmity nor anger. . . without protest and without conscience. . . . an innocent evil" (26-27). Such thoughts are later expressed by Hardayal. He feels more and more that he is a mercenary – in fact, if not in name – and in such circumstances he concludes that so-called "loyalty" to the British commanders rings hollow. His growing discomfort in this matter becomes the dominant issue in the last third of the novel. In the background stands the example of Cawnpore, the Indian Rebellion ("Sepoy Mutiny") of 1857 – Maharani Lakshmi Bai, Nana Saheb (a.k.a Dhondu Pant), Kunwar Singh, Tatya Tope (a.k.a Ram Chandra Pandurang), and Rao Tula Ram. Among the documents related to the incident is A. Dashe's letter of 1858, in which he recommends that the whole village to which an alleged mutineer belongs be given a heavy fine because, as he puts it, "even with the very greatest care, I find it is not always possible to hang the right man. And this is a difficulty which will increase as time goes on" (Dashe: 183).

Beyond that emotional Victorian incident that ramifies in Indian history, questions of loyalty to one's "true" identity present themselves to one character after another in the book. Dinu's half-brother Ilongo, for example, might be seen as a symbol for the developing questions in the book that have to do with hybridity, with crossing over borders – in fact, with interrogating "borders" within oneself, and between peoples. How does one group of people relate to another? *The Shadow Lines* arises out of the emotional impact of this very issue, especially as expressed in the Partition and grandmother's mystification by the apparent lack of any differentiation on either side of the new national lines. How do families blend and merge and separate over time? *In An Antique Land* finds its narrator fascinated by the family history of Ben Yiju as members of the family travel from India to Aden to Sicily, losing track of each other, falling out of history. More so at the point in the book where Ilongo's identity is revealed – that is, the point at which Arjun and Hardayal are questioning their loyalties – how does one *choose* to align himself or herself with a particular identity? When does one allow blood to determine an identity? *The Calcutta Chromosome* is built around an imaginative way to break these traditional blood ties and find personal identity in some less determined location, something beyond place and history.

Hardayal and other Indians in the British army, for example, are beginning to question borders that had hitherto been unquestioned but that now, in the face of imminent slaughter, seem increasingly arbitrary. "Didn't you ever think," he asks Arjun, "this country whose safety, honour and welfare are to come first, always and every time –

what is it? Where is this country? The fact is that you and I don't have a country" (287). Arjun starts to thinking about the pride he felt when he was accepted as an officer for the British, raising him up from the common Indian in the service. For a moment he thinks of his own lowly "batman," his military assistant, and wonders if in fact this lower class Indian has more in common with Arjun than do the British officers who had until then seemed to be his true comrades: "For an eerie instant Arjun saw himself in Kishan Singh's place: as a batman kneeling before a dinner-jacketed officer, buffing his shoes, reaching into his trousers to tuck in his shirt, checking his fly buttons, looking up from the shelter of his parted feet, asking for protection. He gritted his teeth" (289). *Why* did he grit his teeth? Determination never to be placed in so lowly a position? Anger at himself for enabling the humiliation of a fellow Indian? Perhaps both, since he is very conflicted at this point in the book.

When Arjun's battalion arrives in Singapore on its way up the Malay peninsula, he has the sort of experience that another Indian officer had predicted: "it was as though they were examining their own circumstances for the first time, in retrospect; as though the shock of travel had displaced an indifference that had been inculcated in them since their earliest childhood" (300). In short, they are suddenly recognising that they are poor, and that they have never been accepted as equals by the British. Soon he begins listening more closely when Hardayal complains to him:

> It's strange to be sitting in a trench, holding a gun and asking yourself: Who is this weapon really aimed at? Am I being tricked into pointing it at myself? . . . This is what I ask myself, Arjun: In what way do I become human

again? How do I connect what I do with what I want, in my heart? (351)

While he is recuperating in the storm-drain with Kishan Singh, Arjun is impressed by this uneducated man's comparatively clearer understanding of their insignificance in the face of larger historical forces, and he becomes unhinged:

> Was it possible – even hypothetically – that his life [Arjun's], his choices, had always been moulded by fears of which he himself was unaware? . . . Then it would follow that he had never acted of his own volition; never had a moment of true self-consciousness. Everything he had ever assumed about himself was a lie, an illusion. And if this were so, how was he to find himself now? (372)

When Arjun decides to join Hardayal's "mutiny," he wonders:

> Was this how a mutiny was sparked? In a moment of heedlessness, so that one became a stranger to the person one had been a moment before? Or was it the other way around? That this was when one recognised the stranger that one had always been to oneself; that all one's loyalties and beliefs had been misplaced? (380)

It is a question that Ghosh would have us pose – and the reader is left wondering how closely Ghosh would align himself with Arjun's answer. Arjun's ultimate fate further complicates what we might think at this point in the book. Ghosh would have us imaginatively identify with the moment when we may have reached a critical mass of questions that challenge our concept of self – when, for example (to take an extreme case), a member of a religious cult has been confronted again and again with inconsistencies in the rationale of the organisation, and the

The Ebb and Flow of Peoples...

"other" side of the issue suddenly seems less threatening and, in fact, takes on an aura of actual liberation. What is that psychological moment like, when one can suddenly identify with the enemy – and claim it as oneself? The moment, perhaps, of conversion, rather than of "mutiny"?

When Hardayal goes in search of Arjun in June of 1942, he is at first shaken by Arjun's disaffection from the British and his dedication to his new cause:

> This is the greatest danger, he thought, this point at which Arjun has arrived – where, in resisting the powers that form us, we allow them to gain control of all meaning; this is their moment of victory: it is in this way that they inflict their final and more terrible defeat. For Arjun now he felt not pity but compassion. (447)

But he had finally concluded that for him to offer such a pat summation of Arjun's life was far too simplistic and self-satisfied. After all, many had gone the same route. The narrator notes that "when Singapore fell, there were some fifty-five thousand Indian troops on the island. Of these more than half joined the Indian National Army" (448). In fact, Ghosh leads us back to Arjun's decision-making process, in which he had begun to see life through the eyes of the dispossessed, and to view himself through their long-suffering lives. In her interview with him, Michelle Caswell reminded Ghosh that Meenakshi Mukherjee, writing in *The Hindu*, had called *The Glass Palace* "the most scathing critique of British colonialism [she had] ever come across in fiction." Ghosh responded that "if this is true, then it would have to be said, surely, that colonialism has had a pretty easy ride." Nonetheless, all sorts of empires come under criticism within the pages of this novel. One very good critic recognises that

> ... the novel is, in some senses, an elegy for the diasporic condition that is a product of history. ... the diasporic condition that Ghosh mourns. It is the condition that tears one apart, that pits uneven – perhaps incomparable – forces against one another, and then actually makes one choose. (Bose, 2003: 23-24)

Of course, one sometimes does not have the luxury of choice. Even among the diaspora, there are generational differences that Makarand Paranjape discusses: the older generation could never return to the mother land, since travel was difficult, expensive, time-consuming, and this led to a greater rootedness in the new country. Younger generations, though, since they were more cosmopolitan, could "indulge" in a sense of double consciousness, nurtured by trips to the mother land. Ironically, that younger generation might have the greater anxiety regarding choice, since it was pressed by elements in both the old and the new place of residence.

Lingering in the hospital while her son convalesces, Dolly becomes very quiet and introspective, listening to other mothers crying over their dead children:

> ... she'd found herself listening to voices that were inaudible during the day: the murmurs of anxious relatives; distant screams of pain; women keening in bereavement. It was as though the walls turned porous in the stillness of the night, flooding her room with an unseen tide of defeat and suffering. ... She'd begun to cry – it was as though her voice had merged with that of the unknown woman: as though an invisible link had arisen between all of them – her, Dinu, the dead child, his mother. (181-82)

She had learned compassion. This is the sort of internal exploration to which the opening epigraph of the chapter refers: Dolly's interior growth is at least as significant in this novel as is the invasion of Burma itself. The compassion breaks

The Hungry Tide

> [T]o date we do not know what is going to take the place of the nation state. Ideally it would be something like the EU; realistically, in most places it's probably going to be more like the fusion that occurred between southern Afghanistan and Pakistan over the last decade – a world of porous borders, warlords and trafficking in everything available. So it seems right now that we are in a moment when the future is still unborn and the past is not quite dead. (Interview with Rahul Sagar for *The Hindu*, 16 December 2001))

The Story

The book begins with forty-two-year-old Kanai Dutt, who oversees an office of translators in New Delhi. He is standing on a railway platform observing Piyali Roy. When they end up in the same train compartment, he engages her in conversation. They are both heading from Calcutta to Canning in the Sundarbans. He had been there once for a few months in 1970 when he was a young schoolboy, sent to live with his aunt and uncle to "rusticate" him and settle him down for schoolwork. His one friend from that time was a girl in her mid-teens named Kusum. But that was long ago, and the current trip was to be his first return visit. The motivation of his trip after all these years is a bit of a mystery to him: he is going because his aunt Nilima told him that his uncle Nirmal had left a journal specifically for Kanai's eyes only. Although the journal had been written a long time before, in 1979 (the year, in fact, that his uncle had died) it had only recently been discovered in some remote part of the house.

His compartment mate, Piya, had been born in Calcutta, but had moved to the United States when she was just one year old. She did not know Bengali, but she recalls that this is the language in which her parents had argued. She is now a graduate student in cetology at the Scripps Institution of Oceanography in California, and on this trip is interested in observing the marine mammals that she thinks are unique to the Sundarbans. Her destination is the town of Canning, the train stop for that region. Kanai's real destination, on the other hand, is Lusibari, the farthest of the inhabited islands, where his seventy-six-year-old aunt runs a charitable organisation called the Badabon Trust.

Soon after they arrive in Canning, Piya hires a dubious guide and an even more dubious "guard" imposed upon her by the governmental functionaries. The two men soon become quite threatening to this solitary young woman. More immediately, they approach and intimidate a poor fisherman whom Piya had hoped could direct her to the dolphins she wishes to study. In the process she falls into the river and the fisherman, named Fokir, saves her from drowning in the silty, vegetation-filled water. She pays her "helpers" to leave her with Fokir, who promises to take her to the dolphin region. Fokir does not know English, but they manage to do the best they can to communicate.

We learn that the Badabon Trust that Nilima Bose now runs, and the high school that her husband Nirmal had run until his death, were built over the site of a commune established by a British idealist named Sir Daniel Hamilton. The house is called "Lusibari," a pidgin version of "Lucy's House," and was so named for Hamilton's wife who had sadly died on her way from England to join him. Hamilton was a utopian visionary, and he had bought ten thousand acres of the Sundarbans and invited impoverished people to come and populate the place, free to them on one condition – there would be no caste system, and no tribal nationalisms. Despite the crocodiles, tigers, snakes, and dangerous tides, despite the fact that they were farmers and would now have to become fishermen, many desperately poor people heeded his call and arrived. They moved to his commune in three waves – in the 1920s, in 1947 after Partition, and in 1971 after the Bangladesh war – and they helped Hamilton establish a semi-communist region where the in habitants shared possessions.

In 1950, eleven years after Hamilton's death, Nirmal and Nilima Bose had come to Lusibari. They had been married for less than a year, and the reasons for their decision to move to this remote and tenuous locale were complicated. The year before, Nirmal had attended the conference convened in Calcutta of the Socialist International; he had been teaching at Ashutosh College at the time. Nilima was one of his students; her grandfather had been a founding member of the Congress Party, and her father was an eminent barrister at the Calcutta High Court. Although her family did not approve of this marriage, they nonetheless helped arrange the move so that the two could take over management of Hamilton's estate. When the couple arrived, though, they saw utter destitution: much had fallen into decrepitude in the last eleven years. The Hamilton Estate was also crippled by lawsuits. Not an individual who was easily defeated, Nilima established the Women's Union and sought support from outside. By the 1980s, this had developed into the Badabon Trust. It had become, in short, her life's work – though not, perhaps, her husband's.

Kanai learns that his friend from his visit as a child, Kusum, had been abandoned by her mother, who had been tricked into working at a brothel and who had finally been literally worked to death there. In her mother's absence, and to save her from the same fate, the Women's Union had raised Kusum. She had eventually married Rajen, a poor man who had been made lame by a bus in Calcutta. Rajen had taken Kusum to see her mother in the brothel, and her mother had died three months after the two had married in her presence. The couple had a son and they named him Fokir, but just four years after the child's birth, Rajen falls in front of a train and dies.

Almost as if to offer her son someone to take his father's place, Kusum tells Fokir the story of Bon Bibi, a good spirit who fights with the evil spirit Dokkhin Rai for control of the forests and waterways. In the story, there is a man named Dhona who is seduced by the evil spirit into offering a young lad named Dukhey as food to Dokkhin Rai, who sometimes takes the form of a tiger. But Bon Bibi saves Dukhey at the last minute. Kusum was passing on this legend from her own childhood memories. Her father had built a little temple in Bon Bibi's honour on the island of Garjontola, and her son Fokir – and, later, he and his own son Tutul – often visit there. The story has a strong and lasting effect, therefore, on her, her child Fokir, and her grandson Tutul, but Kusum sadly admits that Bon Bibi had not helped her years before, (when Kusum had called out to save her own father, from whom she had learned the legend), from a tiger. In fact, soon after passing along the story to Fokir, Kusum herself abandons him. This is because she had been told by her friend Horen that Dilip, the man who had forced her mother into a life of prostitution, was now hunting for her – hoping to force Kusum to take her mother's place.

Nirmal writes his journal – the one that has now been bequeathed to Kanai – in the village of Morichjhapi the year after his retirement as headmaster. All through her years of establishing the Badabon Trust, his wife had thought he was a writer; in fact, however, the journal is the first and last thing he has written since coming to Lusibari. In it, he is reassessing his life, which he thinks has been a failure, and reassessing his marriage, which he thinks has been overshadowed by his wife's dedication to the Trust and her dismissal of his leftist idealism in favour of her own pragmatism. Nirmal had gone to Morichjhapi to find Kusum. He wanted to warn her of the danger facing the Bangladeshi refugees who had recently fled to Morichjhapi from the resettlement camp in central India to which they had been sent. Morichjhapi was a tiger preserve, and the government considered the refugees to be squatters. When he reaches them in their dangerous and shifting region, Nirmal is won over to their cause. Kusum takes Nirmal to Garjontola, where the Bon Bobi shrine is. During the time that he has been protecting Kusum from Dilip, Horen has fallen in love with her. He now proposes marriage to her and they have sexual relations, but the next, day she is killed in a massacre perpetrated by the government against the "squatters." Her son, Fokir, is just five or six at the time.

The events of the journal, of course, have taken place a good many years before the events of the immediate story in the novel. In the present time, Kusum's son Fokir is an adult, and is married to Moyna. Moyna is a very determined young woman who has managed to give herself an education. She wants to go to nursing school, but her family balks at the idea of her leaving them for further schooling. Their response to her desire had been to force her to marry Fokir. When he first meets her, Kanai immediately admires Moyna for her determination and ambition. Piya, meanwhile, hires Fokir to take her out to observe the dolphins for several weeks.

Horen and Kanai accompany them, and go off on their own for a while. Before he and Horen can get very far, though, Kanai senses that a cyclone is approaching. They also learn that Piya and Fokir have gone out in Fokir's dangerously small boat. As the storm approaches, Horen decides that he can wait for the two of them no longer, and he and Kanai return to Lusibari. Meanwhile, Fokir has steered to Garjontola – in what amounts to a tender instinct handed on to him by his mother, and laden with the hope of Bon Bibi's intervention on behalf of the poor – and he and Piya climb the highest mangrove tree and tie themselves to the trunk. The storm is soon upon them, pausing only momentarily before hitting them repeatedly with full force, followed by a massive tidal wave. Eventually, it subsides. When all has become quiet, Piya sees that Fokir has died in shielding her from the lashing. As he was dying, he was whispering his wife's and son's names to Piya.

Fokir is cremated. A few days pass. Kanai returns to New Delhi, and then Piya reads the letter he has left for her. In it, he admits he understands himself very poorly, and he says he wishes her happiness. He leaves her a full translation of the Bon Bibi legend as a way to understand better Fokir's spirituality and his struggles in his short life, and as an invitation to her to understand that, in differing ways, she was loved by both men. She knows that she had been drawn towards both of them, as if human relations reflected the ebb and tide, the mix of fresh water and salt water, of the Sundarbans.

Piya leaves for a month, but then returns to work at the Badabon Trust. She has set her sights on raising money to see to it that Nilima's dreams will live on – first, by financing a house for Moyna and a college education for her son, Tutul. Piya has decided that she will also move the Trust in the direction of conservation of the endangered dolphins, in consultation with the local fishermen. She can commemorate Fokir, as well, because her Global Positioning System had recorded all the ins and outs of her many days of exploration in the Sundarban waterways with him. She inadvertently calls Nilima's house her "home," suggesting that she no longer wishes to wander, but can now set down roots – even in this unlikely spot with its two daily tides. And Kanai is soon returning to write out what he remembers from reading Nirmal's journal. The book ends, in fact, perhaps a bit too happily for most readers – haunted, as we are, by the spirit of Fokir.

Themes and Concerns

If much of Ghosh's writing meditates on the arbitrary and vexing nature of national borders, this book is surely obsessed with more personal divisions between men and women. One of the major elements of this novel's plot is the story of Kanai's growing relationship with Piya.

Another is Piya's developing understanding of Fokir. A third is Kanai's gradual transformation through his reading of his uncle's account of the "Morichjhapi incident" from some thirty years ago. After *The Glass Palace*'s complex family structure stretching over several generations, *The Hungry Tide* seems almost intimate. Nonetheless, it shares Ghosh's concern for the individual against a broader historical – or even, in this case, geographical – backdrop. The book is divided into two sections – The Ebb, and The Flood – and is set in the Sundarbans. Measuring over ten thousand square kilometres, this delta is the world's largest mangrove ecosystem. The name means "beautiful forest" and is located in the northern part of the Bay of Bengal. It stretches across coastal India and Bangladesh, from the Hooghly River in West Bengal to the shores of the Meghna in Bangladesh. It is the home of the Bengal tiger, which has killed tens of thousands of people. Because the tiger is an endangered species, the government has taken steps to preserve its natural environment. This, however, has resulted in confrontations with the local populace, and that conflict is part of the history behind this novel. The tide comes in twice daily, resulting in a constant reshaping of the land and an uprooting of anything permanent. Such a setting makes an apt symbol for the ebb and flow of history and the uprooting of populations, both of which have come to be seen as "Ghosh-ian" themes. Furthermore, just as the natural tides of the area tend to obliterate the sense of permanent division between land and sea, Ghosh's characters gradually learn to recognise the transient nature of the divisions between individuals – of whatever social class.

Piya and Fokir are kept apart by language and class and by the social institution of marriage; Nirmal and Nilima live side by side for years but are unknown to each other, divided by different dreams for their lives, and by a lack of respect for the other's way of embracing life. This aged couple is, in fact, reminiscent of the first one we have discussed: that of Balaram and his wife in *The Circle of Reason*. Recall how she was driven to distraction by Balaram's obsessions, and then imagine Nilima's words in her mouth:

> It was for your sake that we first came to Lusibari, because your political involvements got you into trouble and endangered your health. There was nothing for me here, no family, friends or a job. But over the years I've built something . . .All these years, you've sat back and judged me. (214)

We must remember, as well, how far Piya has come, because of Fokir's generosity throughout, since she begins as a great sceptic of relationships, reading them through her own experience of her parents' relationship:

> . . .the two of them, Fokir and herself, they could have been boulders or trees for all they knew of each other: and wasn't it better in a way, more honest, that they could not speak? For if you compared it to the ways in which dolphins' echoes mirrored the world, speech was only a bag of tricks that fooled you into believing that you could see through the eyes of another being. (159)

Note how Piya describes her proposed multi-year project in the Sundarbans: "it would be as fine a piece of descriptive science as any. It would be enough; as an alibi for a life, it would do; she would not need to apologise for how she had spent her time on this earth" (127) – what a sad view of life, and what a perfect way to avoid human relationships! "As with many of her peers, she had been drawn to field biology as much for the life it offered as for its intellectual content – because it allowed her to be on her own, to have no fixed address, to be far from the familiar, while still being a part of a loyal but loose-knit community"(126). And yet, how different she is at the novel's end.

Sagarika Ghose writes of this novel that the setting evokes a series of paradoxes in the interaction of these characters:

> Piya learns to love [Fokir] without language. Kanai, the translator of cultures, finds himself stripped down of all urban defences facing a tiger in a swamp. Fokir, the unlettered fisherman, falls in love with a woman who is an embodiment of science [Piya]. A massive storm brings death and terminates a potentially rich love. Nirmal falls in love with Kusum and finally breaks with his armchair past. Ghosh's musings on language, on translatability, on the forgotten massacre of Morichjhapi, in which dominant cultures forcibly wipe out movements from below, are deftly woven into the interactions between the characters. Yet the most dominant theme is of a great sweep away by water, the flood on land, the revolution in the mind. As the reigning deity of the tide country Bon Bibi, in Ghosh's vision a plural syncretic local cult, presides over this flood; she is a goddess of hope but also of vengeance.

The last point is certainly true: the cyclone is powerfully described and reminds readers very forcefully of the humility that is demanded in the face of nature, and our place in it. If much of Ghosh's writing career has demonstrated a fascination with the passage of history, and its continuities over time, this novel seems more to underscore the fragility of our brief time on earth.

This emphasis on the tenuous nature of human existence offers a powerful context for the book's concentrated focus on characters like Fokir who come into life and pass away without rippling the waves of official history. As far as the records are concerned, they are simply among the legions of unimportant individuals like Alu in *The Circle of Reason*, Bomma in *In An Antique Land*, Laakhan in *The Calcutta Chromosome*, grandmother's poor relations in *The Shadow Lines*, or Kishan Singh in *The Glass Palace*. They are voiceless nobodies. Yet Ghosh spills a lot of ink on their behalf, as if to record their personal histories with as much vigor and detail as he did in recovering his own childhood memories in *The Shadow Lines*.

Since Fokir first appears on the scene as something of a knight in shining armor saving Piya from the two "guides," the reader valorises this subaltern character as an honest, possibly complex, figure. Although the squatters of Morichjhapi did not envision themselves as revolutionaries, the poet Nirmal finds them to be extraordinary:

> ...between what was happening at Morichjhapi and what Daniel Hamilton had done there was one vital aspect of difference: this was not one man's vision. This dream had been dreamt by the very people who were trying to make it real.... how astonishing it was that I, an ageing, bookish schoolmaster, should live to see this, an experiment, imagined not by those with learning and power, but by those without. (171)

Theirs is, in effect, a revolution "from below," and they become for Nirmal the subaltern consciousness that he has been seeking all his life. Nirmal describes Kusum, meanwhile, as the muse he never had, representing to him both poetry and revolution. Such "unhistorical" individuals apparently have a capacity to change the lives of those who meet them, since they view the world through quite different eyes.

Crossing the water on their way to the shrine, for example, Kusum tells Nirmal that they had just crossed the border between the realm of humans, protected by Bon Bobi, and the realm of the evil Dokkhin Rai and his demons. There is an eerie echo of *The Shadow Lines* here, as Nirmal suddenly recognises the "imagined" nature of *all* such borders:

> I realised, with a sense of shock, that this chimerical line was, to her and to Horen, as real as a barbed-wire fence might be to me.... To me, a townsman, the tide country's jungle was an emptiness, a place where time stood still: I saw now that this was an illusion, that exactly the opposite was true. (223-24)

Advanced as he is in years, he can still empathise and imagine the world through a pair of eyes very different from his own. He finds himself identifying with the refugees, who refuse to budge and who shout in unison to the onrushing police, "Who are we? We are the dispossessed."

Nirmal first responds by acknowledging the universal yearning of the wretched of the earth, the millions without a home:

> How strange it was to hear this plaintive cry wafting across the water. It seemed at that moment, not to be a shout of defiance, but rather a question being addressed to the very heavens, not just for themselves, but on behalf of a bewildered humankind. Who, indeed, are we? Where do we belong? (254)

But the longer he listens, the more he hears the question as one arising from not only the poor, but from all humanity – and, indeed, from himself:

> [I]t was as if I were hearing the deepest uncertainties of my heart being spoken to the rivers and the tides. Who

was I? Where did I belong? In Kolkata or in the tide country? In India or across the border? In prose or in poetry? ... Where else could you belong, except in the place you refused to leave. I joined my feeble voice to theirs. (254)

His experience parallels that of Arjun in *The Glass Palace*. Sure of himself as well-situated in following the English, Arjun ultimately throws all that overboard when he honestly *sees* the world through the eyes of the less-advantaged Kishan Singh. Nirmal, similarly, now recognises how alienated he had been through most of his life, and how appropriate it now felt to see the world through the eyes of these desperately poor refugees and the uneducated Kusum.

All of this is revealed in the journal that Kanai alone has been allowed to read. Nirmal sounds remarkably like the narrator that we heard at the end of *The Shadow Lines*, who wanted to make sure his memories were not erased, and so he wrote them down. Nirmal seems to have had a similar motivation in writing his journal: "No one knows better than I," he notes, "how skilful the tide country is in silting over its past... perhaps I can make sure at least that what happened here leaves some trace, some hold upon the memory of the world" (69). One need not leap very far to discern in Kanai's words some hint of the motivation that drives a good bit of Amitav Ghosh's writing.

But Kanai makes this observation early in the novel, and he is still standing on the outside as an observer. As the story proceeds, the reader begins to recognise that Kanai and Piya are entering into an experience that might be read as a quest for their souls – a journey in which their minds, finely tuned, are no longer adequate in the face of the Sundarbans. Kanai is forty-two and single, a resident of New Delhi who is a translator and interpreter by profession: in effect, he makes one person understood by another, and yet he does not understand himself. Ghosh is explicit about Piya in this regard, noting (through her mind) that "she had no more idea of what her own place was in the great scheme of things than she did of" people she did not know (35). Like many other fine novelists, in setting the book in this very strange spot, Ghosh has found a metaphor that represents an erasure of the border between what is familiar and what is uncanny, and he invites into it a man of letters and a woman of science. Neither has the armour needed to ward off the monster that awaits them both.

Kanai initially identifies with Moyna and her strong will: "Her ambition was so plainly written on her face that Kanai was assailed by the kind of tenderness we sometimes feel when we come across childhood pictures of ourselves – photographs that reveal all-too-unguardedly the desires people spend lifetimes in learning to dissimulate" (135). As it happens, this is the mirror image of the insight Nirmal had had, years before, into the cynical Calcutta officials – some of whom he had known in college – when they visited Morichjhapi to negotiate the evacuation of the refugees: "[The official] laughed, in the cynical way of those who, having never believed in the ideals they once professed, imagine that no one else had done so either" (192).

Piya, who feels drawn to Fokir and senses female hostility from Moyna, has a different insight into Moyna and Kanai's need for her. She thinks that Moyna, with her ambition, confirms for Kanai the approach he has taken to his own life. As Piya puts it, "It was important for him to believe that his values were, at bottom, egalitarian, liberal, meritocratic" (219). By this logic, even the poorest of the poor can lift themselves up by their own bootstraps, given the requisite willpower. Conversely, "this was a looking-glass in which a man like Fokir could never be anything other than a figure glimpsed through a rear-view mirror, a rapidly diminishing presence, a ghost from the perpetual past that was Lusibari." Yet, Piya recognises that Fokir, far more than Moyna, embodies the dominant spirit of Lusibari and forgotten places like it – countries "full of these ghosts, these unseen presences whose murmurings could never quite be silenced no matter how loud you spoke" (220).

We have seen enough of Ghosh's insights into his characters by now to realise that he is siding with Piya here. One suspects that Kanai needs the same sort of epiphany that Nirmal had earlier experienced. Piya, young as she is, instinctively understands that Fokir, inscrutable and practically speechless, somehow lives directly and immediately – and this is what Kanai cannot yet do.

Serving as Piya's guide, Fokir ties his small boat to Horen's larger one and, with Kanai accompanying them as translator, the four head out. When they near land, they see a large group of people in a circle. Approaching, they see that a tiger is in the centre and the mob is frantically trying to kill it, first with spears and then with fire. Piya and company learn that the tiger had recently killed a new-born calf. Piya objects, and tries to stop them. She has to be dragged away from the angry mob by Fokir and Horen – she seems, in fact, reminiscent of May Price in the face of the Dhaka mob in *The Shadow Lines*, and like May she is oblivious to the danger in which she is putting everyone by romantically standing before a "force of nature." Later, Piya and Kanai remember the scene in a way very suggestive of *The Heart of Darkness* and Marlowe's recollection of the Congo. Piya remarks that "It was like something from some other time – before recorded history. I feel like I'll never be able to get my mind around the—....[t]he horror" (300). To which Kanai intriguingly responds: "aren't we a part of the horror as well? You and me and people like us?" (300)).

As insightful as Piya may be in assessing Kanai's needs, she may not yet realise her own – she cannot "get [her] mind" around it, because it is not a matter of mind. Kanai, in the passage above, may be as insightful in "reading" her as she is in understanding his narrow view of Fokir.

Kanai does not have long to wait for his own psychic encounter with his strengths and weaknesses. Fokir and Kanai are alone in his small boat, and they see the tracks of a tiger on the nearby shore. In a test of manhood, the two dare each other to go ashore. Kanai loses his footing in the mud and needs Fokir's help to get out, but resists asking for it. In fact, he expresses anger "with an atavistic explosiveness" that embodies "the master's suspicion of the menial; the pride of caste" (326). The tables have been turned on this man of the city, whose clients sometimes "were literally 'beside themselves'" (326) with anger when he could not translate a phrase to their satisfaction:

> [It] was just that his job sometimes made him a proxy for the inscrutability of life itself. Yet, despite his knowledge of the phenomenon, he was powerless to stop the torrent of obscenities that were pouring out of his mouth now. (326)

Here he was, facing the "inscrutability of life" himself, and Fokir refused to "translate" for him. In fact, Fokir casts off from shore and leaves Kanai behind. Kanai panics and runs headlong into the mangrove forest, cutting his feet and finally imagines that he sees a tiger stalking him. When Horen returns for him, Kanai is a chastened man who decides to leave the next day for New Delhi. That, of course, is not the end of the story for him. He does not stay in the known world of the city very long before he recognises the pull of the Sundarbans, and returns. This is a remarkably altered man from the one who cynically accepted his aunt's invitation to visit and read his uncle's mysterious journal.

Comparisons might be made between this novel and Herman Melville's *Moby Dick*, of course – a novel similarly obsessed with a mysterious animal that has been read as a symbol of all sorts. For this novel, the Irrawaddy dolphin (*Orcaella fluminalis*) that Piya has come to study reveals itself as a symbol of an original unity. Like many good symbols it takes on various meanings depending upon the one who considers it. It is rumoured to be Bon Bibi's messenger. For Nirmal, it represents the "gaze of the Poet" (235). A poet would, of course, see it in those terms. For Fokir and his family, it would represent their faith in a supportive force beyond the destructive forces that threaten them each day, a kind and intervening mother that wards off the evil that would otherwise wipe them off from the earth. For Piya, who remembers the Indian language that she now hears around her as the language in which her parents argued, it represents the peace of a family that can be pieced together from those around her. That, of course, is why she chooses this unlikely spot as her home. Nirmal had learned much the same thing among the refugees:

> Standing on the deck of the bhotbhoti, I was struck by the beauty of this. Where else could you belong, except in the place you refused to leave. I joined my feeble voice to theirs: 'Morichjhapi chharbona!'. (254)

Common Themes in the Three Novels

What we have seen in the books discussed in this chapter is Ghosh's abiding interest in crossing borders and, in his most recent novel, his ironic obliteration of them. As he has Nirmal tell the five-year-old Fokir, rather ominously: the crabs are eating away at the dikes, and sooner or later the tides will cover the land – "because the animals [quoting Rilke] 'already know by instinct / we're not comfortably at home / in our translated world'" (206). From the book's opening, we already know why Ghosh has chosen such an unusual setting for this novel: the Sundarbans are presented as being borderless, a "utopia" in its original meaning of no-place, where one's familiar markers for identity are constantly shifting. First, according to Hamilton's rules "it was impossible to tell who was who, and what their castes and religions and beliefs were" (79). Then, from a natural point of view, "There [were] no borders here to divide fresh water from salt, river from sea" (7). Ghosh is interested in what might be called imaginary geographies – his preoccupation in *The Shadow Lines* comes to the fore again here – when Piya remarks that she "could tell that the world Kanai inhabited was as distant from the India of her father's memories as it was from Lusibari and the tide country" (200). Brinda Bose nicely sums it up for us:

> As he travels between cultures/lands that diasporas straddle (India/Bangladesh/England in *The Shadow Lines*;

> India/Egypt in *In An Antique Land*; India/Burma/Malaya in *The Glass Palace*) the burden of India's colonial past appears to weigh heavily on a migrant postcolonial generation, and Ghosh seems to be constantly in search of that elusive epiphanic moment in which individuals may come to terms with their histories, thereby releasing themselves from the metaphoric – and metaphysical – burden of their condition . . . . In Ghosh's fiction, the diasporic entity continuously negotiates between two lands, separated by both time and space – history and geography – and attempts to define the present through a nuanced understanding of the past. (Bose, 2003: 17, 19)

In our discussion of these three books, we have noted that they are about Indians living in other countries. In them, Ghosh is more focused on personal lives than on the massive historical sweep that serves as backdrop. Nonetheless, they show his deepening interest in history, time, and memory, almost as though the French autobiographical novelist Marcel Proust had been transplanted to Calcutta.

5. Subaltern Agency as Fiction or Science

The Calcutta Chromosome

> I think it's a pity that science fiction always seeks to project into the future: it's just as interesting to project into the past. (Ghosh, in an interview with Kincaid)

The Story

This book begins with a poem by Sir Ronald Ross (1857-1932), who received the Nobel Prize for Medicine in 1902 for his discovery of the mosquito as a vector for malaria. The poem reads as follows:

> This day relenting God
>   Hath placed within my hand
> A wondrous thing; and God
>   Be praised. At His Command,
>
> Seeking His secret deeds
>   With tears and toiling breath,
> I find thy cunning seeds,
>   O million-murdering Death.

It sets the book's ominous tone early on – the need to search, the religious realm impinging on the secular, the "seeds" of death that are secretly planted. We return to Ross later on, but the action of the book begins in New York in sometime not too far into the future, on August 20 – identified simply as "Mosquito Day." We later learn that this was the day, in 1897, that Ross made his

Subaltern Agency as Fiction or Science

momentous discovery of the malaria parasite in the blood of an Indian named Husein Khan. Meanwhile, however, we are in New York in the twenty-first century, and in the apartment of Antar, a programmer and systems analyst at the International Water Council (formerly LifeWatch) who generally works from home. His retirement is just a year away, and then he plans to return to his native Egypt. He works, therefore, at some leisure at home with the help of his snazzy computer system, named the AVA/IIe, or simply Ava. The computer comes equipped with a powerful search engine, and Antar has asked Ava to see what "she" can do to fill in the blanks on a company identification card that has been partially destroyed. As he waits for the read-out, his mind wanders back to his childhood in his little hamlet on the western edge of the Nile delta, when an old woman, apparently Hungarian and apparently an archaeologist, had spent several months sifting through the sands and looking for something. They had called her al-Magari, and she had sometimes paid Antar and his brothers a bit of money to help her in the search. Continuing his musing, he recalls that he was fourteen when he had left his village and had moved to Cairo, and that it was from there that he had later attended Patrice Lumumba University in Moscow. He is suddenly interrupted in this mental journey through his memories by Ava, who spits out the first bit of information: the missing information from the corrupted ID had been found in Calcutta.

Actually, Antar regrets that he has started Ava on this search, since he had hoped to quit work and get ready for the dinner visit of his neighbour, Tara, an Indian who had moved into a flat on his floor a few months before. Maria, Antar's Guyanese friend, knew that the apartment down the hall from Antar was empty, and she also thought Antar might like a little companionship (Antar's wife had died long ago in her final week of pregnancy) – so she had recommended the place to her friend, Tara. And now Ava spits out another piece of the puzzle: the name on the card is L. Murugan. Suddenly Antar's memory is jostled by this tidbit: he recalls that just a few years before, he himself had typed that name on some company form. He was recording, as he now remembers, the fact that L. Murugan, who had been working for LifeWatch, had disappeared in Calcutta on August 21, 1995 – interestingly, the day after Ross's so-called Mosquito Day, though Antar is unaware of it, at this point in the novel.

As we have seen, it is typical for Ghosh to move through several time periods in his novels – and we now shift back several years, to just one day before Murugan (known in the United States simply as "Morgan") went missing. There he is, in Calcutta, and we find him in front of the memorial to Ronald Ross in front of the Presidency General Hospital. He is, it turns out, a bit of an amateur sleuth and medical historian, and as a hobby has made himself the world's expert on Ross and his research into malaria. When it starts raining, he takes refuge inside the hospital. He overhears the voice of the famous writer, Phulboni, coming across the loudspeaker, and then he encounters two fascinating women: Sonali Das, tall and elegant and mature, and Urmila Roy, recently graduated from college. They are both journalists working for *The Calcutta*. They are here to cover a literary celebration of Phulboni's eighty-fifth birthday. As the two women engage in conversation, it turns out that Urmila Roy recalls the day she met the far-more-famous Sonali Das. It had taken place in Dutton's nursery for plants, where the two had literally bumped into each other. Sonali at that time had been accompanied by Romen Haldar, a wealthy builder and contractor. The woman who oversaw the nursery, a rather intimidating Mrs. Aratounian, had subsequently become friends with young Urmila, and she now suggests that the young reporter interview Sonali Das about some of Phulboni's early stories. (Among these stories, we later learn, the most remarkable are those centering about a character called Laakhan who assumes different identities from one story to the next.) Why Mrs. Aratounian makes the suggestion does not become clear until later in the novel, but it strikes Urmila as a fine idea. With all the hubbub and bother caused by the sudden downpour, however, there is little time for the interview. Sonali therefore invites Urmila to come to her apartment later, and she indicates that Urmila will also thereby get a chance to meet Romen Haldar. Sonali and Romen live together.

When Urmila later accompanies Sonali to Haldar's flat, he is mysteriously missing. The boy he had taken in as a cook is also gone. They decide to wait for him, because this absence is quite unusual, and while they are waiting, Sonali reveals that Phulboni is, in fact, her estranged father. As he had aged, he had become increasingly reclusive. This strange behaviour seemed somehow connected to some secret about "the Silence." He had confided it only once to his wife and they had never discussed it further, but from that point on he began avoiding her – and everyone else. Sonali's mother, though, had passed along the secret to her, and Sonali now shares it with Urmila. It begins with a trip Phulboni makes to Renupur in 1933, when he is a representative of a British firm that makes soaps. By a strange set of circumstances, he ends up having to spend the night alone in the deserted railway station of that remote village, and lives to regret his decision to get off the train in such inhospitable surroundings. He is bored and wanders around, and chances upon a bizarre little shrine with the imprint of a left hand with four fingers and no thumb. As it becomes dark, he goes outside and soon encounters a phantom train that appears apparently from nowhere and disappears just as mysteriously – and then he hears a shout "Laakhan!" from the darkness. At this point in the story he passes out. In the morning the cheery stationmaster (who had been anything but cheery the night before) explains that a young lad named Laakhan had, for years, lived in the station's signal-room, and he had had a deformed hand. He had finally found a home at Sealdah Station, where he had been befriended by a woman. The meaning of the story, at this point, remains vague.

Tired of waiting, Sonali calls Haldar's secretary and learns that Haldar had been suddenly called away, but the nature of the emergency is unknown. On his appointment schedule, however, is an unusual notation to stop the next day at Urmila Roy's family home, of all places, where he is apparently going to see about intervening on Urmila's brother's behalf in his application for a job. Time passes, and Urmila finally decides to go home. At one in the morning Sonali, now somewhat desperate, goes out in search of Romen, and begins with the Ronald Ross mansion that she recalls Romen had been renovating. When she enters the large home, she smells incense and crawls through the dark hallways to a very large living room. She quietly makes her way up to the orchestra balcony, and witnesses a strange ritual going on down below. It appears to involve a young boy and people from all social categories. They sit in concentric circles surrounding an old woman.

She seems to be conducting a sacrifice of some sort, involving a pigeon and, in the centre, a human body. The old woman chants, "The time is here, pray that all goes well for our Laakhan, once again" (167). To her utter amazement and horror, Sonali recognises the body in the centre as that of Romen Haldar, and she faints dead away.

Urmila knows nothing of all this, of course. The next morning, a young boy appears at her door, offering to sell her fish. Urmila's mother had demanded that she stay home from work that day and prepare fish for Romen Halder's visit, so she purchases the boy's offering. He quickly disappears and, in a cascading series of odd events, she discovers that the fish has been wrapped in a page of *The Colonial Services Gazette* from January, 1898. It announces the transfer of one D. D. Cunningham of the British Army Medical Services back to England, to be replaced by one Ronald Ross. She senses that someone is trying to offer her pieces of some puzzle, and she feels a sense of urgency to query Sonali about the deepening sense of coincidence and mystery. Not finding Sonali at home, she guesses that she may have gone off to the Ross mansion. On her way there, she bumps into the man she had met briefly during the outpour, L. Murugan, and she enlists his help.

This, again, is quite serendipitous, since Murugan knows all about the D. D. Cunningham briefly mentioned in the fish wrapping. Murugan looks at the *Gazette* information and realises that something must have deeply frightened Cunningham for him to have given up his laboratory for Ross. As with most people who have arcane hobbies, he welcomes the opportunity to provide Urmila with the full history. He speaks of a connection to Egypt, a fourteen-year-old boy whose blood harboured a special parasite, and a Hungarian woman who went there to investigate something for a Society of Spiritualists. He tells Urmila about a Mme Salminen and Valentinian cosmology, in which the ultimate deities are the Abyss and the Silence, and the cult's belief that the lost "shrine of Silence" was somewhere in Egypt. He suggests that someone is trying to communicate with *him* through Urmila, and he startles her with his apparently paranoid conclusions, suggesting that tantalizing tidbits have been left in the way of carefully chosen individuals throughout the ages – a cascading of details that awaits a catalyst before the full meaning manifests itself:

> But for that to happen two things have to coincide precisely: the end credits have to come up at exactly the same instant that the story is revealed to whoever they're keeping it for. (218)

As insane as this account sounds to her, it does remind Urmila of something she had recently read in Phulboni's writings: "I have never known . . . whether life lies in words or in images, in speech or sight. Does a story come to be in the words that I conjure out of my mind or does it live already, somewhere, enshrined in mud and clay – in an image, that is, in the crafted mimicry of life?" (228). She does not know how this may or may not be connected to Murugan's bizarre account of some mystical sect, but she senses that there is enough plausibility in what he is saying that she shivers at the ominous possibilities.

Sensing her openness, Murugan unleashes on her his pet theory of what it was that Ross was really working on, without his having been aware of his doing so: something Murugan calls the "Calcutta chromosome," unique because "it simply isn't present in regenerative tissue. It only exists in non-regenerating tissue: in other words, the brain.... For what we have here is a biological expression of human traits that is neither inherited from the immediate gene pool nor transmitted into it" (250). Not wanting to tilt him over into some angry outburst, she tentatively asks him why he is so obsessed with this investigation. It had, admittedly, advanced beyond a mere hobby. He admits to her that he has syphilis. He had become intrigued by malaria because he had learned that some doctors intentionally infected syphilitic victims with malaria as a cure for this kind of disease – and he had undergone the procedure. It had cured him, he says, but had done things to his head that he could not fully explain. Now fully engaged in his quest, Urmila rushes with him to Ross' mansion, and there they find a completely disoriented Sonali. She tells them not only that Romen was involved in the ritual, but also that the old woman leading the others, the woman in the centre of the rings, was Mrs. Aratounian – not only the woman who ran the nursery and encouraged Urmila's interest in Phulboni, but also Murugan's landlady. Urmila and Murugan return quickly to his apartment, and find that Mrs. Aratounian and her possessions are completely gone – not only that, the contents of his own apartment have been transported, as well. This triggers a change in Murugan, as if the last necessary piece of data has fallen into place. He has a sudden epiphany, and kneels before Urmila, announcing that she is the chosen one, the one that Mangala has chosen as her next vessel.

Meanwhile, back in the twenty-first century, Antar recalls that he did, in fact, meet Murugan once, back in 1995. Murugan had apparently applied for a transfer from New York to the Calcutta office of the company, and Antar had been asked to discourage him in the attempt. So here we are, back in 1995 at that meeting: over several hours, Murugan gives Antar more than an earful of his theories regarding Ross and the "unacknowledged" conspiracy. Among the minutiae of information regarding Ross that Murugan had accumulated in his studies is the historical fact that we know he later told Urmila: that malaria had sometimes been introduced into patients to help cure syphilis, back when there was no other treatment for the disease. Murugan concludes from this that, "fact is, malaria does stuff to the brain that we're still just guessing at" (55). The careful reader takes this as a hint that some other demonstration of this fact may be forthcoming. He also takes note when he is told that malaria is "just about the most prevalent disease on the planet" (55) and that "it can mimic the symptoms of more diseases than you can begin to count" (56). Murugan tells Antar his pet theory regarding Ross, an apparently paranoid belief in an "Other Mind": "a theory that some person or persons had systematically interfered with Ronald Ross's experiments to push malaria research in certain directions while leading it away from others" (37). For his troubles, Murugan notes, he was laughed at by the scientific community and his theory was ignored. He goes on to give Antar the history of the study of malaria and the other scientific pursuits, some only tangentially relevant, and how they all came fortuitously together on "Mosquito Day," when Ross came to his stunning conclusion about how malaria is transmitted. Among those he discusses is Alphonse Laveran, who decided that the cause of malaria is an animal parasite that "grows inside the red blood cell, eating its host and shitting black pigment" (70). Murugan tells of Abdul Kadir, who had malaria and who presented himself to Ross for experimentation. "Over the next couple of months," says Murugan, "Abdul Kadir's blood guides him through all the critical phases of his research" (72). Throughout his historical account, Murugan suggests that none of this is accidental, and that individuals like Abdul Kadir show up on the scene at critical moments to steer the research in a particular direction. Why they might wish to do so is the central mystery of the novel. As Murugan ominously suggests to Antar: "[Ross] thinks he's doing experiments on the malaria parasite. And all the time it's him who *is* the experiment on the malaria parasite" (79).

This launches Murugan into the heart of his theory, which is the notion that there is, beyond science, a "counter-science," which disputes the claim to *know*: "

> ... not making sense is what it's all about – conventional sense, that is. ... [T]o know something is to change it, therefore in knowing something, you've already changed what you think you know so you don't really know it at all: you only know its history. ... [O]ne way of changing something – of effecting a mutation, let's say – is to attempt to know it. (105)

He suspects that all the Ross "experimentation" is someone else's attempt to bring about a particular mutation in a particular mosquito, with an incredible final outcome: "the ultimate transcendence of nature. ... immortality" (107). More specifically, Murugan thinks he has stumbled on a generational experiment in "a technology for interpersonal transference" (107). After the theorising, Murugan continues with his account of the various late-Victorian researchers who had a hand in the malarial research that he now implies has mystical overtones, unknown to the researchers themselves. One is D. D. Cunningham, who operates a lab in Calcutta and is assisted by a boy and a rather scary woman, both of whom he had recruited from the Sealdah railway station, and both of whom were from the remote rural village of Renupur. The woman's name is Mangala. Another researcher, Elijah Farley, comes to the lab to follow a lead on parasites, and is given short shrift by the woman and boy in Cunningham's absence. When he returns and persists, he is finally given the crucial information by Mangala. But in the meantime, he secretly catches a glimpse of a bizarre ritual in the laboratory's backroom, involving the woman, a pigeon, and sacrifice. Soon after that, he is not heard from again.

One of many characters who seem to keep popping up, possibly over several generations but under different guises, is a fellow named Lutchman – who may, in other situations, be "Laakhan" – who may, in fact, also later be "Lucky," from whom Antar buys his newspaper at the Penn railway station in Manhattan. This is where it all gets a bit bizarre and a little foggy — and also where Ghosh is getting to the compelling thematic material of the novel. In Murugan's view, Lutchman is the one who suggests to Ross that it is only a particular kind of mosquito, the anopheles, that is actually important to the transmission of malaria. "As I see it," says Murugan, "[Lutchman] was all over the map, changing names, switching identities" (87). One physical characteristic that identifies him, and that seems to pop up in other individuals over several generations, is his left hand, which has its four fingers, but no thumb. There was, for example, a "Laakhan" who had helped one of the nineteenth-century researchers, and who had disappeared into the night when his identity was looked into too closely. He shared the physical characteristic.

Antar had been unsuccessful in convincing Murugan to stay in New York, and so, in 1995, there Murugan is in Calcutta, overhearing the Phulboni lecture, haphazardly meeting Urmila Roy and Sonali Das, and (how strange!) staying at a guest house run by Mrs. Aratounian. . . . It is near where Ross had done his research, and the place where Ross had lived is now (strangely) being renovated by a Roman Haldar. The night that he arrives in Calcutta, Murugan watches a bit of television news with Mrs. Aratounian, and there sees Phulboni, described by commentators as "our greatest living writer," emotionally and distractedly going on about having once "betrayed the Silence." Mrs. Aratounian gets up and switches it off. That night, in what he takes to be one of his malarial dreams, Murugan thinks he sees faces around his bed, a grey-haired woman, a gap-toothed boy, the net around his bed filled with mosquitoes, and someone reaching in and trapping an engorged mosquito in a test tube. When he wakes up, he finds that his whole body is aflame, covered with bites, and on the floor there is a broken test tube.

Back in the twenty-first century, Antar is reminiscing over the strange memories that Ava has brought back. He remembers that he has an appointment with Tara later, but he is feeling quite feverish – a relapse of the malaria that he, too, has had for many years. He recalls her telling him that a young gap-toothed boy at the Penn railway station kiosk, named Lucky, had steered her in his direction. He asks Ava to connect him to the director of the Water Council's office in Calcutta, and learns from him that L. Murugan's ID card had been retrieved from a mental asylum. Murugan had apparently turned himself in at a railway station at Sealdah. Sensing that the strands of the mystery are quickly coming together, Antar demands that

Ava reveal to him just what it was that happened to Murugan. The computer asks him if he's really sure he wants the knowledge. He responds in the affirmative, puts on the SimVis headgear, and Ava projects a holographic head representative of Murugan. Murugan shows him Tara, who seems vaguely like Urmila Roy; shows him his Guyanese friend Maria (who had introduced him to Tara), who now seems remarkably like Sonali Das. In his malarial fever, he suddenly hears voices all around him. He sighs as they assure him that they are with him, and that they will help him across.

Themes and Concerns

This novel marks something of a shift away from the exploration of personal memories and moves towards a metaphysical exploration of identity itself, suggesting at the same time that history as defined by the educated elites in the world is far less tamed than one might think. Thus, one's sense of self and of one's place in time becomes unhinged as this detective story unfolds. The themes include history, the politics of scientific research, psychological afflictions, technology and memory, among others. Like so many of Ghosh's works, this one is a merging of various generic expectations – science fiction, criminal detection, history, even spiritual meditation.

R. K. Dhawan accurately notes that "Ghosh makes a unique experiment in *The Calcutta Chromosome* by combining various themes and techniques. He amalgamates here literature, science, philosophy, history, psychology and sociology" (Dhawan, 1999: 26). Although this book seems to be a departure from Ghosh's other novels, he tells interviewer Paul Kincaid that what he wanted to do was to "integrate the past and the present," and in this regard, it surely fits the pattern of his other writing. He told the interviewer that he had conceived of the idea of a secret society dedicated to achieving immortality from the Egyptian Gnostics, and anyone who has read *In An Antique Land* will surely hear echoes from that earlier book's Nashawy in the Egyptian village in this novel, and, perhaps, in the mysterious Renupur as well. He won the Arthur C. Clarke Award for science fiction for this novel, and was delighted to have done so: on the one hand, he had been an avid reader of science fiction when he was a boy, and on the other hand, he thinks he may have been the first Indian and, in fact, the first writer from a developing country to have won such an award (though he, of course, includes Satyajit Ray among the science fiction writers that he enjoyed). Nonetheless, science fiction critics do not think of *The Calcutta Chromosome* as a "genre novel" among typical science fiction books. When Paul Kincaid points out two thematic points that could be drawn from the book – "the role of the colonist who exploits but is largely ignorant of local culture and knowledge," and "the very different attitudes to knowledge and research in East and West" – Ghosh confirms such a reading and notes the book's thematic emphases (and implied critique of colonialism) spring immediately from Ronald Ross's own journals. The novel's historical sections, in fact, stick very closely to the actual facts of Ross's record of his experimentation.

Recall Ghosh's interest in forms of knowledge and in translation as a cultural necessity, topics addressed in various of his other books. With that in mind, it is fascinating to hear the author underscore a point he was trying to make in his portrayal of Ross, the late Victorian researcher. Ross's "real achievement," he tells Kincaid, "lay in translating folk knowledge into the language of science. . . . Ross made a major breakthrough in science based upon a very partial acquaintance with folk knowledge. It follows, surely, that someone who was better acquainted with that knowledge would do even better" – a folklorist/biologist or, even better, a subaltern scientist.

Personal interests and family memories that led Ghosh to his other novels play a part in the genesis of this one, as well. He notes that he frequently passed the Ronald Ross memorial in Calcutta several times a week, and in fact had endured a bout with malaria. "It had a profound effect on my thinking about the human body and its relationship with disease," he tells his interviewer. "Malaria was a strange and hallucinatory experience, but not at all frightening. In fact it was in an odd way very comforting." One wonders how many have had a similarly bemused response to the disease – it does strike one as strangely meditative, almost as though he were outside his body observing it. In any event, his experience with the disease set him pondering India's long encounter with it, and of medicine's benighted transformation of it: in response to drugs it has mutated into "the single most deadly disease in the world" (Ghosh in an interview with Kincaid). It was a stroke of genius to choose it as the centrepiece for a novel, and to do so in such a suggestive manner.

John Skinner reviews Ghosh's growing number of novels, each a good bit different than the last, and finds that the novelist "privileges oral performance. . . on both aesthetic and ideological grounds" (8). But there are challenges in this undertaking: "The effect of such sustained orality over so many different fictional genres," writes Skinner, "is to suggest a kind of fissiparous, but democratised, narrative activity: a literal recuperation of voices which might not otherwise have been heard. And from here, it is a short step to . . . a shift from the language of *stories* to the language(s) *of* these stories" (8). This focus on the speaking parts in the books becomes pointedly more complicated by a decision that Ghosh has apparently made some time ago: his focus on a role that "has absorbed Ghosh ever since *The Circle of Reason*: what might be described as restoring narrative agency to the *Coolie*" (Skinner: 13). In his very insightful essay on this novel, Tabish Khair underscores that the main concern of *The Calcutta Chromosome* is "the question of subaltern agency vis-à-vis alienation" (Khair, 2003: 145). But how one might set about doing this in a convincing way does not offer an obvious pathway:

> This confronts us, first of all, with the problem of accounting for and registering the agency of the Coolie and the non-Babu in a language (English) that is seldom, if ever, employed by the Coolie and the non-Babu (and *never* from choice in an ordinary situation). The Babu, so to say, has a monopoly on the 'medium' through which the knowledge of the Coolie and his/her agency (or the lack of it) is 'exchanged' and *created*. How, then, can this agency be expressed? How can the Coolie be constructed in another language, and one that shares a different socio-economic and discursive siting, without depriving him/her of voice and agency? (145)

But why would Ghosh be interested in this voice, in any case? One might say, first, that there is the matter of justice, of granting to the large percentage of the human population that the "subaltern" represents a deserved acknowledgement as an equal. Thinking back to *The Shadow Lines*, R. Radhakrishnan makes a point about different sorts of consciousness that is as applicable to Laakhan and Mangala as it is to the inhabitants of Calcutta in the earlier novel. Tridib and May, you may recall, meet ironically in front of Calcutta's Victoria Memorial building, and they note certain ironies in their doing so. But Radhakrishnan remarks that

> ... any attempt at universalising or allegorising the meaning of their love will have to pass through the gauntlet of political and historical unevenness and asymmetry. Interpellated differentially by colonial modernity, each of them has to compile an inventory of their traces [this terminology is a reference to postcolonialism's precursor, Antonio Gramsci] before they make sense of their relationship.... Still, the notion of the 'voyage within' privileges the West as the site of postcolonial transformations just as in the case of Tridib and May's loverly tryst, it is the Western memorial that is privileged as the agent of historical cathexis. What if the building had been a Muslim mosque, a Hindu temple, an indigenous pre-colonial site? What if the traces to be remembered were to go beyond the aegis of the colonial regime? (Radhakrishnan, 2002: 784, 785)

The Shadow Lines "envisions a cartography that destabilises all regnant regimes and bureaucracies of identity" (787). In the earlier novels, that hegemonic determinant of identity was nationalism; in *The Calcutta Chromosome*, I would suggest, it is caste.

Beyond this matter of justice, though – and this is, perhaps, a hint at why the subaltern is particularly appropriate in a work of science fiction – there is the notion that "non-subaltern" consciousness, if we can be binary for a moment, has not done such a good job of it throughout history, and is in need of new ideas. As one important reader of Ghosh has noted, "it is only on the assumption of a radical misrecognition of the world *as it is* that the subaltern imagination opens up a different space for a new and emerging kind of cathexis between desire and the object of desire: a space for unprecedented coalitions and solidarities" (Radhakrishnan, 2002: 787). It is the great charm of *The Calcutta Chromosome*, unique among "conspiracy" types of science fiction, that the secret is held by an "alien" presence that is not so alien, after all. What is more, the secret knowledge that they have tortuously accumulated over the centuries is not really a Gnostic cult's private reserve, but is accessible by individuals chosen regardless of class.

Khair also analyses how Ghosh, in this novel, deals with the stereotype of the "irrationality" of colonised peoples, and he does so by focusing on the scene that causes Sonali to faint:

> Tellingly, the climax of the novel is a scene that, in colonial discourses of Indian irrationality, would be described as a scene of 'human sacrifice.' The human sacrifice is probably the most extreme metaphor of non-European (whether Indian or 'Red Indian') otherness. In colonial and even certain neo-imperial discourses, it stands as the example par excellence of the other as mindless, herd-like, barbarous and irrational. In *The Calcutta Chromosome*, significantly, the 'human sacrifice' is taken over and re-inscribed within the subaltern's agency and the subaltern's (suggested) discourses. From that perspective, it becomes a form of discovery, of furthering life and of planned, purposive activity. It becomes in a way the exact opposite of what 'barbaric' and 'irrational' stand for – a planned means of personal improvement and collective wellbeing" (Khair 2003: 149-50).

The purpose of the conspiracy, after all, has nothing to do with world dominance, the production of a new weapon, the accumulation of a massive fortune. Indeed, it seeks the same thing that most spiritual movements throughout time have sought: without using the terminology, the novel seems to be a meditation on the scientific prospects for the transmigration of the soul. As Murugan puts it, "information could be transmitted chromosomally, from body to body. . . . when your body fails you, you leave it, you migrate – you or at least a matching symptomology of your self". In short, "a technology that lets you improve on yourself in your next incarnation" (*The Calcutta Chromosome*: 109).

The secret history of the manipulation of Western malaria researchers also subverts another "given" of colonial theory: the incomprehensibility of the other. Through the Mangala/Laakhan story "'narrative agency' is . . . returned to the colonial subaltern with a vengeance: and this is not agency through the Babu circles, the agency of getting assimilated by European discourses, of becoming 'rational' or 'civilised' (these Manichean concepts do not exist in the novel anyway). The subalterns are from outside the Babu circles" (Khair, 2003: 151). Furthermore, that subtext undercuts the colonial notion of the subcontinent's lack of history, since "in *The Calcutta Chromosome*, Ghosh presents a complex India that achieves coherence on a non-colonial (not Eurocentric, that is) and non-Babu level . . . [since] Ghosh's 'chromosome' suggests a coherence-of-parts which is neither a nationalist 'United' nor based on hegemonic and parochially 'universal' discourses emanating from Europe or from Babu realms of activity" (Khair, 2003: 153-54). In short, though this is science fiction and situated somewhere not-too-far in the future, it is, in fact, an implied rewriting of history, suggesting, as he has in so many of his other works, that there may well have been a lot going on throughout the centuries that the history-book writers just decided to

Subaltern Agency as Fiction or Science 163

overlook. That is the very realm that draws Ghosh to its doorstep, again and again. The epitaph to chapter three was as follows: "It follows then that the reason why I – and many others who have written of such events – are compelled to look back in sorrow is because we cannot look ahead." ("The Greatest Sorrow," *The Imam and the Indian*:317). The epitaph to this current chapter is as follows: "I think it's a pity that science fiction always seeks to project into the future: it's just as interesting to project into the past." (Ghosh in an interview with Kincaid). His immediate reaction to the 9/11 events comes, therefore, as no great surprise: on the morning of the attack, as it happens, he was about to take his eight-year-old son to his first day at a new school. His ten-year-old daughter was already at her school. Then, he received a phone call from his wife, who was already at her office in mid-town Manhattan. He rushed to pick up his daughter.

> Downtown Brooklyn was choked with people and in the distance we saw a plume of dust rising into the clear blue sky, darkening the horizon like a thundercloud. Everyone was heading away from the river; only the two of us seemed to be walking towards the darkness in the distance. ("The Greatest Sorrow,": 322)

There is some talk of turning this book into a film, to be directed by Gabriel Salvatores. The mind reels.

6. BEYOND THE COMMONWEALTH

AMITAV GHOSH AND CONTEMPORARY INDIAN WRITING IN ENGLISH

> Weaving *is* Reason, which makes the world mad and makes it human.... it is a technique for laying a cross-thread ... between parallel long threads..., so that they lock the weft in place. (*The Circle of Reason*, 58, 74)

> It is when we think of the world the aesthetic of indifference might bring into being that we recognise the urgency of remembering the stories we have not written ("The Ghosts of Mrs. Gandhi," *The Imam and the Indian:* 62).

If the first quote reminds us of the joy Amitav Ghosh takes in telling his interlocking stories, the second striking quote underscores the sense of vocation that he brings to the task. We must note, first of all, that writing is a career he chose after, or in the course of, an academic career as a trained anthropologist with a doctorate from a good school. If his novels and essays show strong evidence of that anthropological training – in their careful observation of their characters, surroundings, and history; their implied comparative sweep of cultures and eras; their implied philosophical investigation of what it means to be a human being – they just as strongly show the novelist's delight in narrative, in character development, in themes and symbols and the other stylistic devices that might seem extraneous to strict academic investigation. In short,

Ghosh ties his wagon to imagination, and especially to stories. The second quote, though, forcefully suggests that he retains the anthropologist's dedication to "remembering" stories that otherwise slip from consciousness and from recorded history. Clearly, the act of re-membering, piecing history back together from its disjointed pieces, is intended in Ghosh's works to move readers beyond the "aesthetic of indifference" that might content a lesser novelist who sets out simply to entertain and divert his or her audience from the world's enduring problems. As Brinda Bose astutely observes, he has a "keen understanding... of the political, historical, sociological and cultural nuances of his subjects... and [it] is this sensibility that sets him apart from the clutch of Indian novelists in English that are springing from the woodwork ever since Rushdie immortalised the genre" (Bose, 2003: 18-19). His works do seem pre-eminently immersed in history, and in not only the politics of recent decades, but those of earlier times as well. R. K. Dhawan concludes that "Amitav Ghosh is perhaps the finest writer among those who were born out of the post-*Midnight's Children* revolution in Indian English fiction" (Dhawan: 11).

And what of his own sense of who he is, and what he is doing as a writer? In 1997, in one of many events noting the fiftieth anniversary of India's birth as a nation, Ghosh was interviewed by Mary Gray Davidson, the producer of the American radio programme "Common Ground." When she asked him how he identified himself, he responded: "I must say, I wish I knew. I mean to me, identity is a kind of, it's really an impossible question. And I never feel at all the compulsion to stand up and say, 'I am this, and nothing else.'" In another interview, this time with *Calcuttaweb*, Ghosh clearly wishes to protect the individuality and artistic freedom of all writers as fiercely as he wishes to "protect" his individual sense of who he is. In both cases, he hopes to avoid simplistic and premature categorisation – any facile restriction of writers to a recognised style of writing with an anticipated set of themes, etc. "Every writer," he suggests, "is an individual and every writer has a right to define their own role." And speaking with Michelle Caswell, he suggests that "the novel is a meta-form that transcends the boundaries that circumscribe other kinds of writing, rendering meaningless the usual workaday distinctions between historian, journalist, anthropologist, etc." Regarding his own choices as a novelist, he tells Sheela Reddy that his fiction has always been about "communities coming unmade or remaking themselves." Yet, despite this broader social backdrop it is focused on the individuals because, otherwise, "when you hold up a mirror to violence, all you see is more violence" – an ambiguous but suggestive phrase, arguably emphasising the *individual* as the important locus for change. He is obviously clearing a space in his definition of his writing so that the term for what he does will happily include anthropology, historical research, fiction, social commentary, and – in a word – the freedom to invent new forms.

For his troubles, he has been offered a good number of awards. *The Circle of Reason* won the Prix Medici Etranger, one of France's top literary awards, and it was named a Notable Book of Year (1987) by the *New York Times*. In 1990, he won the Sahitya Akademi Award, India's most prestigious annual literary prize, as well as the Ananda Puraskar, for *The Shadow Lines*. The *New York Times* named *In An Antique Land* one of its notable books of 1993. The Arthur C. Clarke Award, presented to the best science fiction novel published in Britain, was given to Ghosh in 1997 for *The Calcutta Chromosome*. Clarke lived in Sri Lanka, and one might imagine he was happy to finally have someone from his part of the world named as the recipient of his award. The Pushcart Prize, given for stories, poems and essays published in a literary magazine in the United States, was awarded to Ghosh in 1999 for his essay, "The March of the Novel." He was nominated for the American Society of Magazine Editors Award for Reporting, in 1999, for *Countdown*. *The Glass Palace* received the Grand Prize for Fiction at the Frankfurt International e-Book Awards in 2001, and it was named a notable book of the year by the *Los Angeles Times*, the *New York Times*, and the *Chicago Tribune*.

There will surely be other awards in this prolific writer's future, but there is one that he will definitely *not* be winning. In 2001, Ghosh learned that *The Glass Palace* had been nominated for the Commonwealth Writers' Prize, and had been named as the Eurasia regional winner. This meant that the book would advance to the final stage of the competition. The prize carries an award of ten thousand pounds and has been won in the past by the following Indians: 1994, Best Book Prize, to Vikram Seth for *A Suitable Boy*; 1993, Best First Book Prize, to Githa Hariharan for *The Thousand Faces of the Night*; 1996, Best First Book Prize, to Vikram Chandra for *Red Earth and Pouring Rain*. Previous regional winners from India have been Salman Rushdie (2000), Manju Kapur (1999), Amit Chaudhuri (1992), Shashi Tharoor (1990), I. Allan Sealy (1989), and Nayantara Sahgal (1987). But Ghosh had not been consulted before the book had been nominated (publishers apparently often enter books in various competitions without first conferring with their authors), and it subsequently became clear that, had he been asked, he would have requested that the book not be entered into competition. When he learned that he had been nominated and had reached the final stage of judging, he simply requested that the book be withdrawn from the competition. The impact on the literary community was rather dramatic and became something of a *cause celebre*.

In his note declining inclusion, he notes that among his objections is that the phrase itself – "Commonwealth Writers" – "anchors an area of contemporary writing not within the realities of the present day, nor within the possibilities of the future, but rather within a disputed aspect of the past." Mulk Raj Anand had once written on related issues, as had Salman Rushdie and others. "As a literary or cultural grouping," Ghosh goes on, "it seems to me that 'the Commonwealth' can only be a misnomer so long as it excludes the many languages that sustain the cultural and literary lives" of the countries that are member states (Ghosh, PEN: 35). Much like the Kenyan novelist Ngugi wa Thiong'o and his decision to write future novels only in the African language of Gikuyu rather than in English, and like the subsequent Asmara declaration that suggested that only native African languages be used by African writers, Ghosh's public stand drew a lot of attention and comment – far more, perhaps, than he may have anticipated or enjoyed. At any rate, he felt compelled to write to several past winners of the award who were his friends, and explain that he was not impugning them for accepting the award, but was simply making a philosophical point that needed to be discussed by South Asians, British literary critics, and other so-called "Commonwealth" writers.

The Commonwealth Foundation responded to Ghosh's decision to opt out by protesting that "the Commonwealth is *not* the British Empire memorialised; and indeed, a few of its members such as Namibia and Mozambique were never British colonies. . . . And the Foundation recognises, respects and values the fact that [English] is not the first language of most of its peoples." The Foundation asserted that the Commonwealth today exists because "54 independent and sovereign countries have voluntarily chosen to belong to this association of nations and find value in their membership, not least that which derives from their common belief in, and subscription to, freedom and democracy." If, however, the Prize is not intended to perpetuate the memory of the British Empire, one might ask why consideration for the Prize is not extended beyond Commonwealth membership to *all* writers in English, as the Booker Prize has considered doing.

In any event, Ghosh told Sundeep Dougal the following about how one might categorise him as a writer:

> I think of myself as an Indian writer in the first instance. By this I mean that my work has its roots in the experience of the people of the Indian sub-continent, at home and abroad. I think I would be uncomfortable with any categorisation of my work that did not acknowledge this. In this sense, 'Indian Writing in English' seems to me to be a perfectly acceptable categorisation of my work.

But what are we to make of the category "Indian Writing in English" itself, which brings in its wake a history of politics and enduring controversy?

Debashish Mukerji points out that "it all began with *Midnight's Children*," the book that had a seminal influence in triggering the boom in Indian writing in

English. And in that boom, it must be said that Amitav Ghosh has played an early and influential role. As Mukerji notes, Rushdie's novel was published in 1981, but it was not until 1985 that "the first of the new crop of novels, Amitav Ghosh's *The Circle of Reason*, appeared." Vikram Seth's *The Golden Gate* was published the next year, and then in 1988, three "near masterpieces" appeared: *The Trotternama* by I. Allan Sealy, *The Shadow Lines* by Ghosh, and *English August: An Indian Story*, by Upamanyu Chatterjee (and, of course, *The Satanic Verses*). Several others appeared in subsequent years, and then in 1996 Ghosh's well-reviewed *The Calcutta Chromosome* was published along with Rohinton Mistry's *A Fine Balance*. Ghosh himself acknowledges his indebtedness to Rushdie, especially in *The Circle of Reason*. But it is also important to note his other precedents. "For many years," for example, he says that

> I read everything of Naipaul's I could lay my hands on; I couldn't have enough of him. I read him with the intimate, appalled attention that one reserves for one's most skilful interlocutors. It was he who first made it possible for me to think of myself as a writer, working in English. ("Ghosts of Mrs. Gandhi," *The Imam and Indian:* 57)

At any event, it is now clear that Amitav Ghosh came along at just the right time to provide early impetus to a movement that, surprising many observers, has prompted a flowering of writing in English in India far more extensive than that produced during the British occupation – a movement that has brought growing international attention and acclaim to the nation. One of the reasons for this happy renaissance has to do with something of a critical mass of those educated at certain schools in India who were well-trained in writing, along with others of their ilk who made up a large reading public for their works. Another reason was the sudden burgeoning of publishers in India interested in producing such works, even if the audience was smaller than that for other Indian languages. Such publishers know that writers in India who use English frequently get very favourable reviews outside the country, but they also have decided that their audience is first and foremost Indian. This has taken a certain courage on the part of these publishers, but Mukerji quotes Meenakshi Mukherjee to the effect that it has begun to pay good dividends.

> 'One indication,' writes Mukherjee, 'is the attitude of the Bengali literary magazines. Earlier the Bengali literary establishment was fairly contemptuous of those who wrote in English. But now, *Desh*, the foremost Bengali literary magazine, claims that Amitav Ghosh, Amit Chaudhuri, Bharati Mukherjee and Upamanyu Chatterjee are 'Bengali' writers!'

Meenakshi Mukherjee writes that Salman Rushdie, in an infamous essay in the June 1997 special edition of *The New Yorker* celebrating India's fiftieth birthday, was wrong about several things. There is much in his statement, though, with which Mukherjee agrees. As she puts it,

> ...an important dimension of literature is that 'it is a means of holding a conversation with the world.' In order to do that one must of course write in a language the world understands. His insistence about 'parochialism being the main vice of the vernacular literature' ('vernacular' is his word, not mine) I would have been happy to disregard, but the fact is that only a writer in English can have the resource and hence the mobility to travel globally at will. Inveterate readers of travel books and indefatigable travellers within India – the Bangla writers for example – can hardly afford to undertake unusual journeys to less-

travelled parts of the world with the sole purpose of writing about them. The economics of the book industry in their languages will not permit such adventures. I am glad therefore that Amitav Ghosh writes in English because otherwise this book [*Dancing in Cambodia*] would not have come into being – a book that dissolves distances in time and space magically to bring new worlds within our reach. (Review of *Dancing in Cambodia, At Large in Burma*)

Some wonder about a cosmopolitan writer's political commitments and involvement in on-site issues in his or her homeland. This is particularly the case, perhaps, since Salman Rushdie came on the scene. As two recent critics write,

> Another important aspect to which Rushdie draws our attention is the interaction of historical and individual forces. In the 1930's, the Indian English novelist was more concerned with national and political and social problems but the novelist of the 1960's shifted the focus to the individual's quest for personal meaning and his existential problems and social relationships. In the 1980's, there is further discernible change. With Rushdie's *Midnight's Children*, novelists were inspired to take up the relationship between national issues and the individual. (Bhatt and Nityanandam, 2001: 9)

In a like-minded essay on "Rushdie's Children" for *The Nation* in 1997, Amitava Kumar first focuses on Arundhati Roy's *The God of Small Things* and Amitav Ghosh's *The Calcutta Chromosome* to acknowledge the "ignorant and self-congratulatory rhetoric of western publishing" that totally ignores Indian novels in other languages. "And yet," he continues, "there is an undeniable force to several new novels written in English by Indian novelists . . . . [So,] how can we frame this writing with issues that join, rather than separate, them from other milieus both in India and the world?" (37). He worries, in reading Ghosh's account of malaria research, that the central Indian figure of L. Murugan "is condemned at the end to syphilitic dementia and the terror of isolation," and he asks the rather daunting question, "is that cringing figure in any sense an approximation of the modern Indian writer in English?" (39). He does not fully answer his question, and does not let Ghosh and Roy off the hook, even while praising their writing. But he says "we need more reports that carry the burden of the present in all its urgency" (40) – more subaltern voices, perhaps, and more direct political engagement in pressing social issues in India.

The Glass Palace brought criticism from some quarters for becoming "too" involved in such issues. Marina Budhos praises the 2001 novel but notes that it is "saturated" with "questions of agency and volition." "The danger in such a novel," she continues, "is that the fiction can become schematic, as characters fulfil a particular facet of history and the balance shifts toward fact and overwhelms the imaginary terrain" (Budhos, 2001: 5). Pico Iyer similarly cautions that "the one theme giving the huge saga a sense of shape and direction is its insistent, highly contemporary attack on empire and the lost souls left behind it. It's as if a revisionist wolf were dressed in imperialist clothing" (Iyer, 2001: 29), because Ghosh uses a Victorian realistic novel format (presumably the imperialist clothing) to "revise" the Victorian accounts of their Empire. "All he is doing, [Ghosh] might say with justice, is rounding out a picture dominated by British accounts, history in this case having been written mainly by the departing losers" (Iyer, 2001: 31). But Iyer is not convinced that the novelist has presented a balanced picture of what Britain was doing in Burma.

These questions of his role as an Indian writer who uses the coloniser's language were clearly on Ghosh's mind when *The Glass Palace* was published. This fact became clear in his interview with Harriet Gilbert when she asked how he felt to be writing in English. "I believe that literature is one of many paths to self-awareness," he responded. "If I am working with an instrument that actually prevents my self-awareness, I have to ask myself, 'what am I doing?' There is a conflict here, I have to acknowledge it and I have to see a way to step past it." But the following year he had apparently decided that, in his case, self-awareness was not being hindered. At the "At Home in the World" literary festival held in Delhi in 2002, the topic was very much on speakers' minds, but Ghosh, writes Rukmini Bhaya Nair, "seemed impatient with these gripes, dismissing the whole 'Indian languages versus English debate' as meaningless and passé. . . . A writer's business was to write, and problematic values could, in his view, be interrogated as effectively through English as through any other 'Indian' language" (Nair, 2003: 165-66). The point here is that in *The Glass Palace*, Ghosh, a very prominent Indian writer in English, has apparently met the test of political engagement.

Thus, it is as an Indian writer in English that Amitav Ghosh is being judged by critics around the world, and especially so by those who have their roots in South Asia. One sometimes senses a tension in South Asian writers who write in English, especially if they spend part of the year in India and part of the year in Britain or the United States or Canada. There seems sometimes an undercurrent coming from critics in India, implying that a "real" Indian would live in India and would probably not write in English (for a fuller discussion of this, see Hawley 2003). Ghosh has found a way of copying with this tension. On the one hand, "Ghosh does not indulge in 'India-bashing' which is the hallmark of much of Rushdie's writing" (Bhatt and Nityanandam 9). On the other hand, he recognises the limitations of romanticising the "essential" India, as: "I think memories are very important for people who leave any place," he remarks to Mary Gray Davidson in an interview for the *Common Ground* radio programme.

> And it's a curious thing, I mean the people who came here [the United States], presumably didn't actually have very good memories of their home countries, otherwise they probably wouldn't have left, you know. But it's curious how once they come here, time works a certain magic and with succeeding generations there becomes almost a kind of invented homeland, which has very little to do with the realities of the homeland, but is a kind of invented thing, which is invented, really, on the streets of New York or in Flushing, or in Boston or wherever. And that's really, it's really their India. And it's relationship with the real India . . . I'm not sure.

Relations with the "real" India, admittedly, were further complicated by the destruction of the World Trade Center in New York. In his 16 December 2001 interview with Rahul Sagar for *The Hindu*, in discussing 9/11, he remarks:

> It's unpalatable but true, that if there is any country that evokes a depth of feeling similar to the US it is India. . . . pursuing its own narrow economic interests, fomenting terrorism and fundamentalism (Punjab, Sri Lanka) when it suits its purposes, suppressing local cultures with its exported forms of entertainment and so on.

Such outspoken views would seem to indicate that Ghosh has enough confidence in his position as an Indian writer that he makes bold to criticise the land of his birth. They also clearly demonstrate the Janus-face of cosmopolitan writers, who must address two readerships. In a 17 July 2000 interview with *Outlook*, when asked about his staying away from "the media circus that's accompanied Indian Writing in English," Ghosh responds:

> It's a liking of privacy and besides, my publisher Ravi Dayal is very old-fashioned – he's not been plugged into the media publicity circuit in India. I feel that suits me, and it suits Ravi. As far as the media and IWE is concerned, I've kind of always felt that I've been outside the machine. Then again, most of the media response to IWE is purely in the house of fiction, and I've been both in and out of the house.

The interviewer asks whether or not his living in two countries – the US and India – adds a measure of "distance" to his writing? "It wouldn't have been possible to write *The Glass Palace* and *Dancing in Cambodia* if I was living in India," Ghosh responds.

> The lack of resources would have been a problem, as would have been the lack of distance. Nayantara Sahgal is right when she says Indian authors who live elsewhere miss the everydayness of Indian reality. [But] to write a book like *The Glass Palace*, you must have distance. A book like this can't be written exclusively for an Indian or a Burmese audience.

In a nutshell, such an observation outlines both the dilemma and the opportunity facing a contemporary Indian writer in English. In describing such a writer's task as a "dilemma," though, we must not overlook its rewards: bringing into the world something that otherwise would not be here. As one of Amitav Ghosh's early narrators puts it, a novelist has his "own secret map of the world, a map of which only [he knows] the keys and the co-ordinates, but which [is] not for that reason any more imaginary than the code of a safe is to a banker" (*The Shadow Lines*: 190-91).

We conclude with an *Aria da Capo*, returning to his first novel. What was said there about one of his most complex characters, Zindi, might as well be said about Ghosh, for the role he has set for himself is much the same as hers:

They had lived through everything Zindi spoke of...yet it was only in her telling that it took shape; changed from mere incidents to a palpable thing, a block of time which was not hours or minutes or days, but something corporeal. ...That was Zindi's power: she could bring together empty air and give it a body just by talking of it (*The Circle of Reason*: 212-13).

Topics for Discussion

The Circle of Reason

- Considering the book's title, how might reason be seen as a central topic in the book? What are its strengths and appeal in today's world, and its limitations as portrayed in the novel? Circularity also plays a large thematic role, contrasted to Bhudeb Roy's strict linear logic. Which appears to be more powerful? More helpful?

- How is chance a factor in the plot? Does it have "significance," or is it merely serendipity?

- How does traditional Indian literature play a part in the book? How does Ghosh use connotations from this earlier writing to enhance his themes?

- Demonstrate the use of magic realism in the book. How helpful would you say these devices are in support of Ghosh's themes? How would you compare them to Salman Rushdie's writing, or to any of the Central and South American writers like Gabriel Garcia Marquez who frequently use similar techniques?

- Is Jyoti Das a necessary character?

- How would you characterise the portrayal of women in this book?

- Discuss the clash of traditional and modern value systems in the book.

Topics for Discusssion

- Does the direction of the flight/quest – westward – have any implications for the theme of this book? What is being sought by the various characters? How successful is each in this quest?

- Is the book hopeful? Humanistic?

- Does the book show evidence of being a first novel?

The Shadow Lines

- How effective was the juggling of time in this novel? What effect does it have on the reading of the book – how does the reader learn about important events, and why is this manipulation of the reader important to the theme?

- How are Ila and the narrator mirror images of each other?

- What does grandmother represent for Ghosh?

- Is Tridib a hero? A fool? A child?

- What do you think of the portrayal of Nick and of May? What roles do they play in the imaginations of the narrator, and Ila, and Tridib? What role does Tridib play in the imaginations of May and of the narrator?

- Discuss the book's portrayal of the border between Dhaka and Calcutta.

- Thematically, what is the importance of the way of seeing that Tridib teaches the narrator?

- What is the book saying about one's memories and one's individual perceptions on reality?

- What other books that you have read deal with similar issues?

- The narrator remarks that "every language assumes a centrality, a fixed and settled point to go away from and come back to, and what my grandmother was looking for was a word for a journey which was not a coming or a going at all; a journey that was a search for precisely that fixed point which permits the proper use of verbs of movement" (150). What does this mean?

- Discuss the differences in the generations in this book.

- What role does the notion of diaspora play in the novel?

- The book ends with May and the narrator in each other's arms: "I stayed, and when we lay in each other's arms quietly, in the night, I could tell that she was glad, and I was glad too, and grateful, for the glimpse she had given me of a final redemptive mystery" (246). How redemptive is that mystery, would you say? What needed redeeming?

- What do you think is the future of the concept of the nation-state in today's world?

- Tridib tells the narrator that everyone lives in a story. What does that mean, and how true is it?

Topics for Discusssion **181**

- Reminiscing about Tridib's death, Robi, Ila, and the narrator offer each other support: "Then Ila, who had been sitting beside him, stood up too and put an arm around his shoulders and another around mine, and held us together. We stood a long time like that, on the steps of that derelict church in Clapham, three children of a free state together, clinging" (242). What is the central irony of that picture?

In An Antique Land

- How effective is the generic experiment that Ghosh has undertaken in this book?

- Do you find any interesting parallels between the objectification of Bomma by Ghosh, and the objectification of Ghosh by the villagers?

- How metaphorical is the "antique land" in which Ghosh finds himself? What commonalities do India and Egypt have, in that regard? What impact does globalization have on such places in the world?

- Do you trust the history presented in this form as being factual? What is the effect of Ghosh surmising various events and reasons regarding Ben Yiju's wife? Is this intentional, or simply sloppy? What are the varying strengths of history and story – and how distinct are the two categories?

- Does it matter, in any way, who Bomma was?

- If you had been one of the villagers in Nashawy, what would you have thought of Ghosh?

- What do you know of the history of trade routes between India and Africa?

- The conversation between Imam Ibrahim and Ghosh startles and depresses Ghosh. Ghosh believes that the Imam and the other villagers had accepted and assimilated the Western Image of them. What do you think of Ghosh's interpretation. (see the very end of the "Nashawy" chapter)?

- The last sentence of the book is: "Nabeel had vanished into the anonymity of History." Does that fact matter?

The Glass Palace

- What do you know about the Long March that Ghosh mentions in this novel?

- What do you think of Rajkumar – his strengths and weaknesses? Can you find evidence in the novel that Ghosh admires this character and/or finds him reprehensible?

- Are we meant to sympathise with the deposed King of Burma?

- For all its importance in the region and in the events framing this novel, Britain plays a rather invisible part in the book. Why is this so?

- Should Ghosh have allowed this book to be put forward for the final round of competition for the Commonwealth Writers' Prize?

Topics for Discusssion 183

- How do the lessons of Shelley's poem "Ozymandias" relate to this novel?
- What classics of Indian literature ramify in this long family history?
- Is this novel another version of *The Shadow Lines*, completely re-imagined from another starting point?
- What do you think of Uma? Of Dolly? Of Supayalat? Of the other female characters?
- Which character did you find most admirable, and why?

The Hungry Tide

- If this is a love story, whose story is it?
- How would you say that "the hungry tide" serves as a metaphor?
- If you have visited this region (the Sundarbans) how accurate is Ghosh's portrayal?
- Did you find Fokir the more admirable or Moyna?
- Do you identify with Kanai?
- Why did Nilima and Nirmal not communicate better with each other? Which was the stronger character?
- What other literary treatments that you know of have used weather as, a central character in the work?

- Discuss the characters in this novel against the backdrop of Ghosh's characters from other novels. What sorts of echoes do you hear?

- Are you convinced by the hopeful ending of the novel? What did you think of Fokir's death? Why didn't Ghosh kill Piya, instead?

The Calcutta Chromosome

- How successfully does the science in this book work? Does it seem accurate to you? Does that make a difference in your involvement with the philosophical issues it raises? What would you say those philosophical issues are?

- There is recent news of progress in the discovery of a malaria vaccine. How has this disease affected human history?

Bibliography

Works by Amitav Ghosh:

Fiction

The Circle of Reason. New Delhi: Ravi Dayal/Permanent Black, 1986.

The Shadow Lines. New York: Penguin, 1988.

In An Antique Land: History in the Guise of a Traveler's Tale. New York: Vintage, 1994 [Knopf, 1993]

The Calcutta Chromosome: A Novel of Fevers, Delirium and Discovery. New York: HarperCollins, 2001 [Avon, 1995].

The Glass Palace. New York: Random House Inc., 2002.

The Hungry Tide. London: HarperCollins, 2004.

Non-fiction

Kinship in Relation to Economic and Social Organization in an Egyptian Village Community. Unpublished doctoral dissertation, Oxford: Bodleian Library, MS D.Phil. c. 4127, 1982.

Dancing in Cambodia, At Large in Burma. Delhi: Ravi Dayal, 1998.

Countdown. Delhi: Ravi Dayal, 1999.

The Imam and the Indian: Prose Pieces. Delhi: Ravi Dayal / Permanent Black, 2002.

Articles, Essays and Short Stories

'The Imam and the Indian'. *Granta: In Trouble Again.* 20 (1986): 135-46.

'Categories of Labour and the Orientation of the Fellah Economy' in Ahmed al-Shahi (ed.) *Peter Lienhardt Festschrift* Oxford: Oxford UP, 1988.

'Tibetan Dinner'. *Granta: Murder.* 25 (1988): 250-54.

'Four Corners'. *Granta: Travel.* 26 (1989): 191-96.

'Pharoahs and Phantoms'. Review of *Egypt, Islam and the Arabs: The Search for Egyptian Nationhood 1900-1930*, by Israel Gershoni and James Janowski. *The New Republic.* 5 June 1989: 33-37.

'The Diaspora in Indian Culture'. *Public Culture.* 2.1 (1989): 73-78.

'The Human Comedy in Cairo: A Review of the Work of Naguib Mafouz'. *The New Republic.* 202 (7 May 1990): 32-36.

'An Egyptian in Baghdad'. *Granta: Death of a Harvard Man.* 34 (1990): 173-93.

'In India, Death and Democracy'. *New York Times.* 26 November 1990, A19.

'Petrofiction: The Oil Encounter and the Novel'. *The New Republic.* 206 (2 March 1992): 29-34.

'The Slave of MS. H.6' in Partha Chatterjee and Gyanendra Pandey (eds.) *Subaltern Studies: Writing on Asian History and Society: VII* New Delhi: Oxford UP, 1992: 159-220.

'Holiday in Cambodia'. *The New Republic.* 208 (28 June 1993): 21-25.

'Dancing in Cambodia'. *Granta: The Last Place on Earth.* 44 (1993): 125-69.

'The Global Reservation: Notes Toward an Ethnography of International Peacekeeping'. *Cultural Anthropology.* 9.3 (1994): 412-22.

'The World of a Bengali-Speaker in New York'. *Observer Magazine* London September, 1993.

'Stories in Stone'. *Observer Magazine* London December, 1993.

'The Indian Story: Notes on Some Preliminaries'. *Civil Lines* New Delhi 1: 35-49.

'The Ghosts of Mrs. Gandhi'. *The New Yorker.* 71 (17 July 1995): 35-41.

'The Fundamentalist Challenge'. *Wilson Quarterly.* 19.2 (1995): 19-31. Reprinted in *The Writer and Religion,* (ed.) William H. Gass and Lorin Cuoco. Carbondale, IL: Southern Illinois UP, 2000: 86-110.

'The Hunger of Stones' (a translation of Rabindranath Tagore's Bengali short story). *Civil Lines* New Delhi 2 (1995): 152-68.

'Fortifications and the Synagogue: The Fortress of Babylon and the Ben Ezra Synagogue'. *American Journal of Archaeology.* 100.4 (1996): 808-809.

'Burma'. *The New Yorker* 12 August 1996: 38-54.

'Empire and Soul: A Review of *The Babarnama*'. *The New Republic.* 6 & 13 January 1997.

'India's Untold War of Independence'. *The New Yorker.* 73 (23 & 30 June 1997): 104-121.

'The March of the Novel Through History: The Testimony of my Grandfather's Bookcase'. *Kunapipi* 19.3

(1997): 2-13. Reprinted in *Kenyon Review.* 20.2 (1998): 13-24.

'Why Can't Every Country Have the Bomb?' *The New Yorker* 26 October and 2 November 1998: 186-97.

'Calcutta's Global Ambassador'. *The New York Times.* 29 June 2000.

'Afterword' in *Burma: Something Went Wrong,* by Chan Chao Tucson: Nazaraeli P, 2000.

'54 University Ave Yangon – Aung San Suu Kyi'. *Kenyon Review.* 23.2 (2001): 158-65.

'The Indian Novel: An Introduction'. *Europe-Revue Litteraire Mensuelle.* 79.864 (2001): 36-45.

'The Magic of Reading V. S. Naipaul: An Adolescent Memoir'. *Europe-Revue Litteraire Mensuelle* 80.873-874 (2002): 293-95.

'Sun: Set: Past Tense'. *PEN America: A Journal for Writers and Readers* 2.3 (2002): 35-36.

'Imperial Temptation'. *Nation.* 274.20 (27 May 2002): 24.

'Satyajit Ray' in Tabish Khair (ed.) *Amitav Ghosh: A Critical Companion* New Delhi: Permanent Black, 2003: 1-8.

'The Greatest Sorrow: Times of Joy Recalled in Wretchedness'. *Kenyon Review.* 25.3-4 (2003): 86-99.

Victoria, Queen. 'Proclamation'. 1 November 1858 in Barbara Harlow and Mia Carter (eds.) *Imperialism and Orientalism: A Documentary Sourcebook* Malden, Massachusetts: Blackwell, 1999: 210.

Viswanathan, Gauri. 'Beyond Orientalism: Syncretism and the Politics of Knowledge'. *Stanford Humanities Review.* 5.1 (1995): 19-34.

Ward, Geoffrey C. and Robert Atwan. (ed.) *The Best American Essays, 1996* Boston: Houghton Mifflin, 1996.

Wassef, Hind. 'Beyond the Divide: History and National Boundaries in the Work of Amitav Ghosh'. *Alif: Journal of Comparative Poetics.* 18 (1998): 75-95.

Weisbord, Merrily. 'Amitav Ghosh'. *College English Review.* 1.4 (1997): 4-5.

Yang, Lingyan. 'Theorizing Asian America'. Diss., University of Massachusetts, 2001.

Young, Robert J.C. *Postcolonialism: A Very Short Introduction* New York: Oxford UP, 2003.

Zaman, Niaz. 'Nostalgic Shadows: The Partition in Sunil Gangopadhyay, Amitav Ghosh, and Taslima Nasreen'. *A Divided Legacy: The Partition in Selected Novels of India, Pakistan and Bangladesh* Dhaka: Manohar Publications, 1999.

Zinkin, Taya. 'Review of *Dancing in Cambodia, At Large in Burma*'. *Asian Affairs.* 30.2 (1999): 230-31.

Interviews:

Aldama, Frederick Luis. 'An Interview with Amitav Ghosh'. *World Literature Today: A Literary Quarterly of the University of Oklahoma* 76.2 (2002): 84-90.

Anon. 'Interview'. http://www.calcuttaweb.com/articles/lahiri1.htm

Anon. 'Coming under Burmese Fire was Surreal'. *Outlook.* 17 July 2000. http://www. outlookindia.com

Caswell, Michelle. 'An Interview with Amitav Ghosh'. *Asia Source.* 6 September 2004. http://www.asiasource.org/arts/ghosh.cfm

Davidson, Mary Gray. 'India at Fifty: Writers Reflect'. *Common Ground* program 9730 29 July 1997. http://www.commongroundradio.org/shows/97/9730.html

Dougal, Sundeep. 'I am not a Person who Seeks out Controversy'. *Outlook.* 22 March 2001. http://www.outlookindia.com

Gilbert, Harriet. 'Ghosh's Words of Change'. 27 July 2000. http://www.bbc.co.uk/worldservice

Kincaid, Paul. 'Ghosh Interview: *The Calcutta Chromosome*'. http://www.appomattox.demon.co.uk/acca/Reviews/ghoshinterview.htm

Mahanta, Banibrata, Somdev Banik and Namrata Rathore. 'Writing is Like Music: Interview with Amitav Ghosh'. *The Hindu.* 21 May 2000.

Reddy, Sheela. 'Amitav Ghosh: Writing Through Turmoil'. (*in Outlook*) 19 August 2002. http://www.worldpress.org

Sagar, Rahul. 'Interview with Amitav Ghosh'. (*in The Hindu*) http://www.amitavghosh.com/articles

—. 'Of Epistemic Upheavals'. *The Hindu.* 16 December 2001. http://www.hindu.com/thehindu/mag/2001

Silva, Niluka and Alex Tickell. 'Amitav Ghosh in Interview'. *Kunapipi* 19.3 (1997): 171-177. Reprinted in Brinda Bose (ed.) *Amitav Ghosh: Critical Perspectives* New Delhi: Pencraft International, 2003. 214-21.

Weisbord, Merrily. 'Amitav Ghosh'. *College English Review* 1.4 (1997): 4-5.

Website:

www.amitavghosh.com

Secondary Works on Ghosh:

Acton, S. M. 'Review of *The Calcutta Chromosome*'. 1998. http://www.silcom.com/~manatee/ghosh_calcutta.html

Adhikari, Madhumalati. 'The *Calcutta Chromosome*: A Post-Colonial Novel' in Indira Bhatt and Indira Nityanandam (eds.) *The Fiction of Amitav Ghosh*: 177-83.

Advani, Rukun. 'Novelists in Residence'. *Seminar.* 384 (1991): 15-18.

Agarwalla, Shyam S. 'Magic Realism in Amitav Ghosh's The Circle of Reason' in Amar Nath Prasad (ed.) *Studies in Indian English Fiction* 2001.

—. '*In an Antique Land*: A Critical Study' in R. K. Dhawan (ed.) *The Novels of Amitav Ghosh*: 164-77.

Ahmed, Kazi Anis. 'In Partition's Shadow: Fictions of Violence and Sovereignty in India'. Diss. New York University, 2004.

Almond, Ian. 'Post-Colonial Melancholy: An Examination of Sadness in Amitav Ghosh's *The Shadow Lines*'. *Orbis Litterarum*. 59.2 (2004): 99-99.

Amin, Armina. 'Going Away/Coming Home: Points of Fixity or *The Shadow Lines*' in Indira Bhatt and Indira Nityanandam (eds.) *The Fiction of Amitav Ghosh*: 50-56.

Andersen, Elizabeth J. 'Excavating the Remains of Empire: War and Postimperial Trauma in the Twentieth-Century Novel'. Diss., University of New Hampshire, 2002.

Anon. 'Amitav Ghosh 1956: Indian novelist, essayist and nonfiction writer'. *Contemporary Literary Criticism*. 153 (2002): 81-132.

Anon. 'An Area of Brightness: The Mystique of Oriental Experience'. http://www.pugmarks.com/week/authors.htm.

Aslami, Zarene. 'Questions of Authority: The Story of Three Generations Living in the Shadow of Empire: Review of *The Glass Palace*'. *Chicago Tribune Books*. 1154.35 (4 February 2001): 3, 7.

Bagchi, Nivedita. 'The Process of Validation in Relation to Materiality and Historical Reconstruction in Amitav Ghosh's *The Shadow Lines*'. *MFS: Modern Fiction Studies* 39.1 (1993): 187-202.

Baker, Phil. 'Post-Colonial Pox: Review of *The Calcutta Chromosome*'. *Times Literary Supplement* (2 August 1996): 23.

Bammer, Angelika. *Displacements: Cultural Identities in Question* Bloomington: Indiana UP, 1994.

Barat, Urbashi. 'Imagination and Reality in *The Shadow Lines*' in R.K. Dhawan (ed.) *The Novels of Amitav Ghosh*: 114-22.

—. 'Time in *The Shadow Lines*' in Indira Bhatt and Indira Nityanandam (eds.) *The Fiction of Amitav Ghosh*: 40-49.

Baravalle, Giorgio and Carl Modine. *Newyorks eptembereleventwothousandone* Mill, NY: F & W Publications, 2001.

Barrett, David. 'Collected Works: A Review of *The Calcutta Chromosome*'. *New Scientist*. 155.2091 (19 July 1997): 48.

Basu, Ranjita. 'Amitav Ghosh's Action: Turning the Full Circle' in Nilufer E. Bharucha and Vrinda Sarang (eds.) *Indian English Fiction 1980-1990*: 151-60.

—. 'The Novels of Amitav Ghosh'. *London Magazine*. 37.3-4 (1997): 159-61.

Basu, Srimati. 'Refracted Light: Teaching *In An Antique Land*': in Brinda Bose (ed.) *Amitav Ghosh*: 204-212.

Basu, Tapan. 'Mimic Missions: *Countdown* as Critique of the Nuclear Arms Race in South Asia' in Brinda Bose (ed.) *Amitav Ghosh*: 155-59.

Batra, Kanika. 'Geographical and Generic Traversings in the Writings of Amitav Ghosh' in Kathleen Gyssels et al (eds.) *Convergences and Interferences*: 211-20.

Bhargava, Rajul. (ed.) *Indian Writing in English: The Last Decade*. New Delhi: Rawat, 2002.

Bharucha Nilufer E. and Vrinda Nabar (eds.) *Mapping Cultural Spaces: Postcolonial Indian Literature in English: Essays in Honour of Nissim Ezekiel* New Delhi: Vision, 1998.

Bhatia, Meetu. 'Amitav Ghosh: Transfiguration of Memory in *The Shadow Lines*' in Rajul Bhargava (ed.) *Indian Writing in English: The Last Decade* New Delhi: Rawat, 2002.

Bhatt, Indira. 'Disappearances and Discovery: A Study of *The Calcutta Chromosome*' in Indira Bhatt and Indira Nityanandam (eds.) *The Fiction of Amitav Ghosh*: 189-96.

Bhatt, Indira and Indira Nityanandam. (eds.) *The Fiction of Amitav Ghosh* New Delhi: Creative Books, 2001.

Bhosh, Bishnupriya. 'When Speaking with Ghosts: Spectral Ethics in *The Calcutta Chromosome*' in Brinda Bose (ed.) *Amitav Ghosh*: 117-38.

Biddick, Kathleen. 'Translating the Foreskin' in Glenn Burger and Steven F. Kruger (eds.) *Queering the Middle Ages. Medieval Cultures 27*: 193-212.

Bose, Brinda. (ed.) *Amitav Ghosh: Critical Perspectives*. Delhi: Pencraft International, 2003.

—. 'Footnoting History: The Diasporic Imagination of Amitav Ghosh' in Makarand Paranjape (ed.) *In Diaspora*: 235-45.

Brawarsky, Sandee. 'Mortality, Mosquitoes, and Mystery: Review of *The Calcutta Chromosome*'. *Lancet*. 348.9043 (21 December 1996). 1717.

Budhos, Marina. 'Questions of Allegiance: Review of *The Glass Palace*'. *Los Angeles Times Book Review*. (11 February 2001): 5.

Buford, Bill. *The Last Place on Earth* New York: Granta, 1993.

—. 'Declarations of Independence: Why are there suddenly so many Indian Novelists?' *The New Yorker*. 23 & 30 June 1997.

Carroll, Clare and Patricia King. *Ireland and Postcolonial Theory* Notre Dame, IN: U of Notre Dame P, 2003.

Chambers, Claire. *The Relationship Between Knowledge and Power in the Work of Amitav Ghosh* Leeds, 2003.

—. 'Historicizing Scientific Reason in Amitav Ghosh's *The Circle of Reason*' in Tabish Khair (ed.) *Amitav Ghosh*: 36-55.

Champeon, Kenneth. 'The Last Queen of Burma'. *The Iriwaddy*. 1 July 2003. http://www.irrawaddy.org

Chandra, Subhash. '*The Calcutta Chromosome*: A Postmodernist Text' in R.K. Dhawan (ed.) *The Novels of Amitav Ghosh*: 265-69.

Chandra, Vinita. *Constructing National Identities: Indo-Anglian Fiction*. Diss., Rutgers University, 1996.

—. 'Suppressed Memory and Forgetting: History and Nationalism in *The Shadow Lines*' in Brinda Bose (ed.) *Amitav Ghosh*: 67-77.

Chatterji, Roma. 'Between Myth and Ethnography: An Anthropological Reading of *In An Antique Land*' in Brinda Bose (ed.) *Amitav Ghosh*: 91-102.

Chaudhuri, Gita. 'The Narrator in *The Shadow Lines*: Coming to Terms with Reality' in Indira Bhatt and Indira Nityanandam (eds.) *The Fiction of Amitav Ghosh*: 93-98.

Chew, Shirley. 'Texts and Worlds in Amitav Ghosh's *In An Antique Land*' in Maureen Bell et al (eds.) *Re-Constructing the Book*: 197-209. Reprinted in 'Texts and Worlds in *In An Antique Land*' in Brinda Bose (ed.) *Amitav Ghosh*: 103-116.

—. 'The Story Bug: Review of *The Calcutta Chromosome*'. *New Statesman* (6 September 1996): 47.

Clifford, James. 'Looking for Bomma'. *London Review of Books*. (24 March 1994): 26-27.

—. 'The Transit Lounge of Culture'. *Times Literary Supplement* (3 May 1991): 7-8.

Commonwealth Foundation. 'Press Release: Commonwealth Writers Prize 2001– Commonwealth Foundation Responds to Author's Withdrawal'. 22 March 2001. http://www.commonwealthfoundation.com/news/news183.html

Couto, Maria. 'Threads and Shards: Review of *The Shadow Lines*'. *Times Literary Supplement*. (28 October-3 November 1988): 1212.

Daiya, Kavita. 'No Home But in Memory': Migrant Bodies and Belongings, Globalization and Nationalism in *The Circle of Reason* and *The Shadow Lines*' in Brinda Bose (ed.) *Amitav Ghosh*: 36-55.

Damor, Nutan. 'Roots of Alienation' in Indira Bhatt and Indira Nityanandam (eds.) *The Fiction of Amitav Ghosh*: 125-32.

Dashe, A. 'Letter on Measures to Suppress the Mutiny in Kiyalpore District' in Barbara Harlow and Mia Carter (eds.) *Imperialism and Orientalism: A Documentary Sourcebook* Malden, Massachusetts: Blackwell, 1999: 181-83.

Davis, Rocio G. 'To Dwell in Travel: Historical Ironies in Amitav Ghosh's *In An Antique Land*' in Gerhard Stilz (ed.) *Missions of Interdependence*: 239-46

Dayal, Samir. 'The Emergence of the Fragile Subject: Amitav Ghosh's *In An Antique Land*' in Monika Fludernik (ed.) *Hybridity and Postcolonialism. ZAA Studies: Language, Literature, and Culture*. 1. Tübingen, Germany: Stauffenburg, 1998: 103-33.

Dhawan, R. K. (ed.) *The Novels of Amitav Ghosh* New Delhi: Prestige, 1999.

Dhingra, Leena. 'Exhumation: A Novel and Critical Commentary'. Diss., University of East Anglia, 2001.

Dixon, Robert. 'Travelling in the West: The Writing of Amitav Ghosh'. *The Journal of Commonwealth Literature.* 31.1 (1996): 3-24

—. 'Travelling in the West: The Writing of Amitav Ghosh' in Tabish Khair (ed.) *Amitav Ghosh: A Critical Companion* Delhi: Permanent Black, 2003: 9-35.

Docker, John. 'His Slave, My Tattoo: Romancing a Lost World' in Debjani Ganguly (ed.) *Unfinished Journeys: India File from Canberra* Adelaide, Australia: CRNLE, 1998: 181-200.

Dodiya, Jaydipsinh Dodiya. (ed.) *Perspectives on Indian English Fiction.* New Delhi: Dominant, 2002

Dubbe, P. D. 'Postcolonial Discourse in Amitav Ghosh's *The Shadow Lines*' in Basavaraj Naikar (ed.) *Indian English Literature: Vol. I* .

Dutta, Pradip. 'A Voice Among Bullet Holes: *The Circle of Reason*' in R.K. Dhawan (ed.) *The Novels of Amitav Ghosh*: 39-45.

Eakambaram, N. 'The Theme of Violence in *The Shadow Lines*' in R.K. Dhawan (ed.) *The Novels of Amitav Ghosh*: 96-104.

Elukin, Jim. 'Cairene Treasures: *In An Antique Land*, An Infidel in Egypt'. *American Scholar* 63.1 (1994): 137-40.

Gandhi, Leela. 'A Choice of Histories: Ghosh vs. Hegel in An Antique Land'. *New Literatures Review* 40 (2003): 17-32.

—. 'A Choice of Histories: Ghosh vs. Hegel in *In An Antique Land*' in Tabish Khair (ed.) *Amitav Ghosh*: 56-72.

—. '*In An Antique Land*: A View' in R.K. Dhawan (ed.) *The Novels of Amitav Ghosh*: 192-93.

Ganguly, Keya. 'Something Like a Snake: Pedagogy and Postcolonial Literature'. *College Literature*. 19-20.3-1(1992 Oct-1993 Feb): 185-90.

Gass, William H. and Lorin Cuoco. *The Writer and Religion*. Carbondale: Southern Illinois UP, 2000.

Geertz, Clifford. 'Review of Amitav Ghosh's *In An Antique Land*'. *The Australian*. (25 August 1993): 30.

—. 'A Passage to India: Amitav Ghosh's *In An Antique Land*'. *New Republic*. 209.8-9 (1993): 38-41.

Gera, Anjali. 'Des Kothay? Amitav Ghosh Tells Old Wives Tales' in Tabish Khair (ed.) *Amitav Ghosh*: 109-127.

Ghose, Sagarika. 'The Shadow Links: Review of *The Hungry Tide*'. *The Indian Express*. 27 June 2004. http://www.indianexpress.com/full_story.php?content_id=49600

Ghosh, Tapan K. 'A Journey to the Unknown: A Quest for Immortality in *The Calcutta Chromosome*' in R.K. Dhawan (ed.) *The Novels of Amitav Ghosh*: 249-56.

—. 'Beyond the 'Shadow Lines': Amitav Ghosh's Quest for the Remnants of an Antique Civlization' in R.K. Dhawan (ed.) *The Novels of Amitav Ghosh*: 151-63.

Ghosh-Schelhorn, Martina. 'Chromosome der Utopie: Utopische Entwhrfe in der anglophonen Literatur Indiens' in Hans-Ulrich Seeber and Ralf Pordzik (eds.)*Utopie und Dystopie in den neuen englischen Literaturen* Heidelberg: Carl Winter, 2002: 275-87.

Gupta, Babli. 'Enigma as Ontology in *The Calcutta Chromosome*' in R.K. Dhawan (ed.) *The Novels of Amitav Ghosh*: 206-218.

Gupta, Nilanjana. '*In An Antique Land*: A Counter-Narrative of Coloniality' in R.K. Dhawan (ed.) *The Novels of Amitav Ghosh*: 194-201.

Gupta, Pallavi. 'Private History, Individual Memory and the Amateur Historian: A Study of *The Shadow Lines*' in Indira Bhatt and Indira Nityanandam (eds.) *The Fiction of Amitav Ghosh*: 75-82.

Gupta, Ramesh Kumer. 'Feverish Fallacy: *The Calcutta Chromosome*' in Indira Bhatt and Indira Nityanandam (eds.) *The Fiction of Amitav Ghosh*: 222-26.

Gupta, Santosh. 'Looking into History: Amitav Ghosh's *The Glass Palace* in Rajul Bhargava (ed.) *Indian Writing in English*.

Hale, Nanette and Tabish Khair. (eds.) *Angles: On the English-Speaking World: Volume 1: Unhinging Hinglish: The Language and Politics of Fiction in English from the Indian Subcontinent* Copenhagen: U of Copenhagen P, 2001.

Harlow, Barbara and Mia Carter. (eds.) *Imperialism and Orientalism: A Documentary Sourcebook* Malden, Massachusetts: Blackwell, 1999.

Hawley, John C. 'Can the Cosmopolitan Speak: The Question of Indian Novelists' Authenticity'. *South Asian Review*. 24.2 (2003): 26-40.

Hayward, Helen. 'Once a Golden Land: Review of *The Glass Palace*'. *Times Literary Supplement*. 5076 (14 July 2000): 21.

Heinz, Antor and Klaus Stierstorfer. (eds.) *English Literatures in International Contexts. Anglistische Forschungen. 283.* Heidelberg, Germany: Carl Winter Universitätsverlag, 2000.

Hemmadi, Usha. 'Amitav Ghosh: A Most Distinctive Voice' in Nilufer E. Bharucha and Vrinda Nabar (eds.) *Mapping Cultural Spaces.*

Henderson, Bill, (ed.) *The Pushcart Prize, 2000, XXIV: Best of the Small Presses* Wainscott, NY: Pushcart, 2000.

Hewett, Heather. 'The Persistence of Memory in Love and War: Review of *The Glass Palace'. Christian Science Monitor.* (8 February 2001): 20.

Hiatt, Shobha. 'Review of *The Calcutta Chromosome'.* 1998. http://www.indolink.com/Book/calcutta.html

Hickling, Alfred. 'Islands in the Stream: Review of *The Hungry Tide'. The Guardian Weekly.* 19 June 2004. http://www.books.guardian.co.uk/print

Holland, Patrick and Graham Huggan. *Tourists with Typewriters: Critical Reflections on Contemporary Travel Writing* Ann Arbor, MI: U of Michigan P, 1999.

Howe, Stephen. 'Sea Changes: Review of *In An Antique Land'. New Statesman and Society.* 25.222 (1992): 48-49.

Hulse, Michael. 'O Death, Where is Thy Bite? Review of *The Calcutta Chromosome'. Spectator* 277.8771 (1996): 25-26.

Hussain, Shawkar. 'Post-Colonial Angst in Amitav Ghosh's *The Shadow Lines'* in Niaz Zaman et al (eds.) *Colonial and Post-Colonial Encounters* Dhaka: Manohar Publications, 1999.

Irwin, Robert. 'Out of the Dustbin of History: Review of *In An Antique Land*'. *Washington Post Book World*. 22.13 (28 March 1993): 6.

Iyer, Pico. 'The Nile of Time: Review of *In An Antique Land*'. *Los Angeles Times Book Review*. (11 April 1993): 2, 11.

—. 'The Road from Mandalay: Review of *The Glass Palace*'. *New York Review of Books*. 48.4 (2001): 28-31.

Jack, Ian. (ed.) *Twenty-One: The Best of Granta Magazine*. London: Granta, 2001.

James, Louis and Jan Shepherd. 'Shadow Lines: Cross-Cultural Perspectives in the Fiction of Amitav Ghosh'. *Commonwealth Essays and Studies*. 14.1 (1991): 28-32.

—. 'Shadow Lines: Cross-Cultural Perspectives in the Fiction of Amitav Ghosh' in R.K. Dhawan (ed.) *The Novels of Amitav Ghosh*: 52-58.

Jones, Stephanie. 'A Novel Genre: Polylingualism and Magical Realism in Amitav Ghosh's *The Circle of Reason*'. *Bulletin of the School of Oriental and African Studies*. 66.3 (2003): 431-41.

Joseph, May and Jennifer Natalya Fink. (eds.) *Performing Hybridity*. Minneapolis: U of Minnesota P, 1999.

Joshi, Priya. 'A Bridge Over Troubled Water: British Popular Fiction and the Development of the Novel in India'. Diss., Columbia University, 1995.

Joshi, Ulka. '*The Circle of Reason*: Caught up in Circles' in Indira Bhatt and Indira Nityanandam (eds.) *The Fiction of Amitav Ghosh*: 25-33.

Kakar, Jolie M. Fareshta. 'Imagined Nation'. M.A. Thesis, San Francisco State University, 2003.

Kamath, Rekha. 'Memory and Discourse: On Amitav Ghosh's *In an Antique Land*' in Thomas Wägenbaur (ed.) *The Poetics of Memory. Stauffenburg Colloquium.* 45, Germany: Stauffenburg, 1998: 205-13.

Kapadia, Novy. (ed.) *Amitav Ghosh's The Shadow Lines: Critical Perspectives* New Delhi: Prestige, 2001.

—. 'The Politics of Isolation and Resurgence in *Dancing in Cambodia, At Large in Burma*' in R.K. Dhawan (ed.) *The Novels of Amitav Ghosh*: 282-94.

Karpe, Anjali. 'The Concept of Freedom in *The Shadow Lines*: A Novel by Amitav Ghosh' in Nilufer E. Bharucha and Vrinda Nabar (eds.) *Mapping Cultural Spaces.*

Kaul, A.N. 'A Reading of *The Shadow Lines*' in *The Shadow Lines*, Delhi: Oxford UP edition, 1995: 299-309.

—. '*The Shadow Lines*'. *Indian Literature*. 33.4 (1990): 88-95.

Kaul, Suvir. 'Separation Anxiety: Growing Up Inter/National in Amitav Ghosh's *The Shadow Lines*'. *Oxford Literary Review* 16.1-2 (1994): 125-45.

Keen, Suzanne. *Romances of the Archive in Contemporary British Fiction* Toronto: U of Toronto P, 2001.

Khair, Tabish. (ed.) *Amitav Ghosh: A Critical Companion.* Delhi: Permanent Black, 2003.

—. *Babu Fictions: Alienation in Contemporary Indian English Novels* Delhi: Oxford UP, 2001.

—. 'Amitav Ghosh's *The Calcutta Chromosome*: The Question of Subaltern Agency' in Tabish Khair (ed.) *Amitav Ghosh*: 142-61.

—. 'The Example of Amitav Ghosh: (Re)Establishing Connections'. *Babu Fictions: Alienation in Contemporary Indian English Novels* New Delhi: Oxford UP, 1995: 302-32.

Khan, A. G. *The Calcutta Chromosome*: A (Counter)-Science Fantasy of Suspense Tantra and Interpersonal Transference' in Indira Bhatt and Indira Nityanandam (eds.) *The Fiction of Amitav Ghosh*: 184-88.

—. 'Book Review: *In An Antique Land* by Amitav Ghosh'. 2000. http://www.metimes.com/2K/issue2000-49/cultent/book_review.htm

Khan, Nyla Ali. 'Transporting the Subject: The Fiction of Nationality in an Era of Transnationalism'. Diss., University of Oklahoma, 2004.

Khatri, C. L. 'The Narrative Technique of Amitav Ghosh's *The Shadow Lines*'. *Zenith: A Literary Magazine.* 7 (2001-2002): 50-55.

—. 'The Narrative Technique of *The Shadow Lines*' in Indira Bhatt and Indira Nityanandam (eds.) *The Fiction of Amitav Ghosh*: 99-106.

Kich, Martin. 'Mosquito Bites and Computer Bytes: Amitav Ghosh's *The Calcutta Chromosome*'. *Notes on Contemporary Literature.* 30.4 (2000): 9-12.

King, Bruce. '*In An Antique Land*'. *World Literature Today.* 68.2 (1994): 430.

Kirpal, Viney. *The New Indian Novel in English: A Study of the 1980s* New Delhi: Allied Publishers Ltd., 1990.

Kiteley, Brian. 'Trapped by Language: On Amitav Ghosh's *In An Antique Land*'. 2000. http://www.du.edu/~bkiteley/ghoshtalk.html

Klinkenborg, Verlyn. 'Life on the Edge: Review of *The Shadow Lines*'. *New Republic* 201.6 (1989): 37-39.

Kothari, Reena. 'A Traveller's Tale: *In An Antique Land*' in Indira Bhatt and Indira Nityanandam (eds.) *The Fiction of Amitav Ghosh*: 107-111.

Kumar, Akshaya. 'Prose Behind and Beyond the Shadow Lines: Review of *The Imam and the Indian*'. *The Tribune of India*. 20 April 2003. http://www.tribuneindia.com/2003/20030420/spectrum/book4.htm

Kumar, Amitava. *Away: The Indian Writer as an Expatriate*. New York: Routledge, 2004.

—. 'Rushdie's Children: Review of *The Calcutta Chromosome*'. *The Nation*. (29 September 1997).

Kumar, Gajendra. '*The Calcutta Chromosome*: A Strange Odyssey of Time and Mystery' in Manmohan K. Bhatnagar and M. Rajeshwar (eds.) *Indian Writings in English, Vol. IX*.

Kumar, Priya. 'Ruptured Nations, Collective Memory and Religious Violence: Mapping a Secularist Ethics in Post-Partition South Asian Literature and Film'. Diss., McGill University [Canada], 2001.

Lal, Vinay. 'A Meditation on History: Review Article on Amitav Ghosh's *In An Antique Land*'. 1993. http://www.sscnet.ucla.edu/southasia/History/British/Amitav_Ghosh.html

Law-Yone, Wendy. *Irrawaddy Tango*. Evanston, IL: Northwestern UP, 2003, 1993.

Leer, Martin. 'Odologia Indica: The Significance of Railways in Anglo-Indian and Indian Fiction in English'. Nanette Hale and Tabish Khair (eds.) *Angles: Volume 1*: 41-61.

Luo, Shao-Pin. 'Translation, Transformation, and Transculturation: A Study of Selected Postcolonial Texts'. Diss., University of New Brunswick [Canada], 1998.

Lutwick, Larry I. 'Review of *The Calcutta Chromosome*'. *Infections in Medicine*. 15.3 (1998): 173.

Macaulay, Thomas Babington. 'Introductory Report upon the Indian Penal Code' in Barbara Harlow and Mia Carter (eds.) *Imperialism and Orientalism*: 74-80.

Majeed, Javed. 'Amitav Ghosh's *In An Antique Land*: The Ethnographer-Historian and the Limits of Irony'. *The Journal of Commonwealth Literature*. 30.2 (1995): 45-55.

Majumdar, Nivedita. 'The Nation and its Discontents: A Critique of Nationalism in South Asian Literature'. Diss., U of Florida, 2003.

Majumdar, Sharmila Guha. '*The Shadow Lines* and *In An Antique Land*: Some Thematic Considerations' in R.K. Dhawan (ed.) *The Novels of Amitav Ghosh*: 178-86.

Malhotra, Meenakshi. 'Gender, Nation, History: Some Observations on Teaching *The Shadow Lines*' in Brinda Bose (ed.) *Amitav Ghosh* Delhi: Pencraft International, 2003: 173-94.

Mani, K. Ratna Sheila. 'Of Lines and Borders: A Reading of Amitav Ghosh's *The Shadow Lines*' in Jaydipsinh Dodiya (ed.) *Perspectives on Indian English Fiction*. New Delhi.

Mee, Jon. '"The Burthen of the Mystery': Imagination and Difference in *The Shadow Lines*" in Tabish Khair (ed.) *Amitav Ghosh: A Critical Companion* Delhi: Permanent Black, 2003: 90-108.

Mhatre, L. 'The Shadow Lines'. Confrontation 44-45 (1990): 414-38.

Mishra, Pankaj. 'Review of The Glass Palace'. New York Times Book Review 106.6 (2001): 7.

Mongia, Padmini. 'Medieval Travel in Postcolonial Times: Amitav Ghosh's In An Antique Land' in Tabish Khair (ed.) Amitav Ghosh: 73-89.

—. 'Postcolonial Identity and Gender Boundaries in Amitav Ghosh's The Shadow Lines'. College Literature. 19-20.3-1. (1992 Oct-1993 Feb): 225-29.

Moral, Rakhee. "'In Time of Breaking of Nations': The Glass Palace as Postcolonial Narrative" in Brinda Bose (ed.) Amitav Ghosh: 139-54.

Mukherjee, Meenakshi. The Perishable Empire: Essays on Indian Writing in English New Delhi: Oxford UP, 2000.

—. 'Maps and Mirrors: Coordinates of Meaning in The Shadow Lines'. The Shadow Lines Delhi: Oxford UP edition, 1995: 255-67.

—. 'In Antique Lands'. Indian Review of Books 7.10 (1998): 6-8.

—. 'Dancing in Cambodia, At Large in Burma'. India Star Review of Books. 1998. http://www.indiastar.com/mukherjee1.html

Naipaul, V. S. The Mimic Men New York: Vintage, 1995 [1967].

Nair, Rukmini Bhaya. 'The Road from Mandalay: Reflections on Amitav Ghosh's The Glass Palace' in Tabish Khair (ed.) Amitav Ghosh: 162-74.

Nayar, Pramod K. 'An Ontology of the Elsewhere: Rhizomatics in The Calcutta Chromosome' in Indira

Bhatt and Indira Nityanandam (eds.) *The Fiction of Amitav Ghosh*: 163-76.

Nelson, Diane M. 'A Social Science Fiction of Fevers, Delirium and Discovery: *The Calcutta Chromosome*, the Colonial Laboratory, and the Postcolonial New Human'. *Science Fiction Studies*. 30.2 (2003): 246-66.

Neogy, Alpana. 'The Partition of Bengal: A Comparative Study of Amitav Ghosh's *The Shadow Lines* and Sunil Gangopadhyay's *Purba Paschim*' in R.K. Dhawan (ed.) *The Novels of Amitav Ghosh*: 81-86.

Nityanandam, Indira. 'A Sense of Space and Time: *The Calcutta Chromosome*' in Indira Bhatt and Indira Nityanandam (eds.) *The Fiction of Amitav Ghosh*: 158-62.

Pandit, Nirzari. 'Subversion of History in / through Fiction: A Study of *The Shadow Lines* and *In An Antique Land*' in Indira Bhatt and Indira Nityanandam (eds.) *The Fiction of Amitav Ghosh*: 133-41.

Panosian, Claire. 'Once Bitten: Review of *The Calcutta Chromosome*'. *Los Angeles Times Book Review*. 21 September 1997: 13.

Papastergiadis, Nikos. *The Turbulence of Migration*. Cambridge: Polity Press, 2000.

Paranjape, Makarand R. *In Diaspora: Theories, Histories, Texts* New Delhi: Indialog Publications, 2001.

Paul, Arunima, Swaati Chattopadhyay, Neha Dixit and Arunima Sengupta. 'A Students' Colloquium on Studying *The Shadow Lines*' in Brinda Bose (ed.) *Amitav Ghosh*: 195-203.

Ponzanesi, Sandra. 'Diasporic Narratives @ Home Pages: The Future as Virtually Located' in Gerhard Stilz (ed.) *Colonies, Missions, Cultures in the English Speaking World*: 396-406.

Prasad, Amar Nath. 'C*ountdown*: A Portrayal of the Dance of Death' in Indira Bhatt and Indira Nityanandam (eds.) *The Fiction of Amitav Ghosh*: 227-37.

Prasad, G. J. V. 'Re-Writing the World: *The Circle of Reason* as the Beginning of the Quest' in Brinda Bose (ed.) *Amitav Ghosh*: 56-66.

—. 'The Unfolding of a Raga: Narrative Structure in *The Circle of Reason*' in Viney Kirpal (ed.) *The New Indian Novel in English*: 101-108.

—. 'Really Imagined'. *Seminar.* 384 (1991): 23-25.

Prasad, Murari. "*The Shadow Lines*: A Quest for 'Indivisible Sanity' " in R.K. Dhawan (ed.) *The Novels of Amitav Ghosh*: 87-95.

Premnath, Gautam. 'Arguments with Nationalism in the Fiction of the Indian Diaspora'. Diss., Brown University, 2003.

Radhakrishnan, R. 'Derivative Discourses and the Problem of Signification'. *European Legacy.* 7.6 (2002): 783-95.

—. *Theory in an Uneven World* Oxford: Blackwell, 2003: 27, 188-89.

Rao, Nagesh. 'Cosmopolitanism, Class and Gender in *The Shadow Lines*'. *South Asian Review* 24.1 (2003): 95-115.

Ravi, P. S. *Modern Indian Fiction: History, Politics and Individual in the Novels of Salman Rushdie, Amitav Ghosh and Upamanyu Chatterjee* New Delhi: Prestige Books, 2003.

Ray, Biswanath. *Socio-Economic Development in India* New Delhi: Mohit Publications, 2001.

Rosenberg, Paul. 'Review of *The Calcutta Chromosome*'. *Christian Science Monitor.* (8 January 1998): 12.

Roy, Anjali. "Microstoria: Indian Nationalism's 'Little Stories' in Amitav Ghosh's *The Shadow Lines*". *Journal of Commonwealth Literature.* 35.2 (2000): 35-49

Rushdie, Salman. *Mirrorwork: 50 Years of Indian Writing, 1947-1997* New York: H. Holt, 1997.

—. *The Vintage Book of Indian Writing, 1947-1997* London: Vintage, 1997.

Sagar, Aparajita. *Fiction on the Indian Subcontinent* Lafayette, IN: Department of English, Purdue University, 1993.

Saint, Tarun K. *Bruised Memories: Communal Violence and the Writer* Calcutta: Seagull Books, 2002.

Schama, Simon, William Boyd, et al. *Death of a Harvard Man* New York: Granta, 1990.

Schulze-Engler, Frank. 'Literature in the Global Ecumene of Modernity: Amitav Ghosh's *The Circle of Reason* and *In An Antique Land*' in Antor Heinz and Klaus Stierstorfer (eds.) *English Literatures in International Contexts*: 373-96.

Schumacher, Lyn. 'Review of *The Calcutta Chromosome*'. *Foundation* 71 (1997): 120-22.

Seeber, Hans-Ulrich and Ralf Pordzik. (eds.) *Utopie und Dystopie in den neuen englischen Literaturen* Heidelberg: Carl Winter, 2002.

Sen, Asha. 'Towards a National Culture? India and its Diasporas'. Diss., Purdue University, 1996.

—. 'Crossing Boundaries in Amitav Ghosh's *The Shadow Lines*'. *Journal of Commonwealth and Postcolonial Studies.* 5.1 (1997): 46-58.

Sen, Sudeep. *'The Calcutta Chromosome'*. *World Literature Today.* 71.1 (1997): 221-22.

Shack, Neville. 'Rational Capers: Review of *The Circle of Reason*'. *Times Literary Supplement.* (11 April 1986). 382.

Shammas, Anton. 'The Once and Future Egypt: Review of *In An Antique Land*'. *New York Times Book Review.* (1 August 1993). Sec. VII. 26.

Sherry, Simon. 'Frontières de la mémoire: La Partition de l'Inde dans *The Shadow Lines* d'Amitav Ghosh'. *Etudes Françaises.* 34.1 (1998): 29-43.

Shohat, Ella. 'Taboo Memories and Diasporic Visions: Columbus, Palestine, and Arab Jews' in May Joseph and Jennifer Natalya Fink (eds.) *Performing Hybridity* Minneapolis: U of Minnesota P, 1999: 131-56.

—. 'Rupture and Return: The Shaping of a Mizrahi Epistemology'. *HAGAR: International Social Science Review.* 2.1 (2001): 61-92.

Siddiqui, Yumna. 'Anxieties of Empire and the Fiction of Intrigue'. Diss., Columbia University, 1999.

—. 'Police and Postcolonial Rationality in Amitav Ghosh's *The Circle of Reason*'. *Cultural Critique.* 50 (2002): 175-211.

Silva, Neluka and Alex Tickell. 'An Interview with Amitav Ghosh' in Brinda Bose (ed.) *Amitav Ghosh*: 214-21.

Singh, Sujala. 'Faithful Representations? Religion, Nation and Identity in South Asian Narratives'. Diss. State University of New York at Stony Brook, 1998.

Singh, Sushila. 'Double Self in Amitav Ghosh's *The Shadow Lines*'. *Language Forum: A Half-Yearly Journal of Language and Literature*. 18.1-2 (1992): 135-42.

Sinha, Nandita. 'Perspectives in Time: The Narrator as Child in *The Shadow Lines*' in R.K. Dhawan (ed.) *The Novels of Amitav Ghosh* New Delhi: Prestige, 1999: 143-48.

Sircar, Ajanta. 'Individualizing History: The 'Real' Self in *The Shadow Lines*'. *Social Scientist*. 19.12 (1991): 33-46.

Sircar, Arjya. 'The Stranger Within: Amitav Ghosh's Quest for Identity'. *Language Forum*. 18.1-2 (1992): 143-47.

Skinner, John. 'Embodying Voices: Language and Representation in Amitav Ghosh's *The Glass Palace*'. *BELL: Belgian Essays on Language and Literature*. (2002): 137-49.

Somtow, S. P. 'Variations on an Indian Theme: Review of *The Shadow Lines*'. *Washington Post Book World*. (16 July 1989): 9.

Soni, J. D. '*The Calcutta Chromosome*: A Miracle of Rare Device' in Indira Bhatt and Indira Nityanandam (eds.) *The Fiction of Amitav Ghosh*: 197-205.

Soueif, Ahdaf. 'Intimately Egyptian: Review of *In An Antique Land*'. *Times Literary Supplement*. (15 January 1993): 7.

Srivastava, Neelam. 'Amitav Ghosh's Ethnographic Fictions: Intertextual Links between *In An Antique Land* and His Doctoral Thesis'. *Journal of Commonwealth Literature*. 36.2 (2001): 45-64.

—. 'Fictions of Nationhood in Amitav Ghosh's *The Shadow Lines*' in Brinda Bose (ed.) *Amitav Ghosh*: 79-90.

Stageman, Mike. 'Innocence Lost: Indo-Anglian Representations of Post-Colonial Identities Through Adolescent Hardships'. Diss., 2001.

Steger, Manfred B. *Globalization: A Very Short Introduction* New York: Oxford UP, 2003.

Gerhard Stilz. (ed.) *Colonies, Missions, Cultures in the English Speaking World: General and Comparative Studies. ZAA Studies: Language Literature Culture 12.* Tübingen, Germany: Stauffenburg, 2001.

Sunder Rajan, Rajeswari. 'The Division of Experience in *The Shadow Lines*'. Preface to *The Shadow Lines* Delhi: Oxford UP edition, 1995: 287-98.

Sudrann, Jean. 'Goings and Comings: Review of *The Shadow Lines*'. *Yale Review.* 79.3 (1990): 414-38.

Swain, S. P. 'The Quest for Meaning: A Study of *The Shadow Lines*' in R.K. Dhawan (ed.) *The Novels of Amitav Ghosh*: 130-35.

Tadie, A. 'Amitav Ghosh: The Nuances of History'. *Esprit* [Paris]1 (2002): 62-73.

Taneja, G. R. '*The Shadow Lines*: A Note' in R.K. Dhawan (ed.) *The Novels of Amitav Ghosh*: 149-50.

—. 'Review of *The Shadow Lines*'. *World Literature Today.* 65.2 (1991): 365.

Thieme, John. 'Passages to England' in Theo D'haen and Hans Bertens (eds.) *Liminal Postmodernisms: The Postmodern, the (Post) Colonial, and the (Post-)Feminist. Postmodern Studies 8* Amsterdam: Rodopi, 1994: 55-78.

—. 'The Discoverer Discovered: Amitav Ghosh's *The Calcutta Chromosome*' in Tabish Khair (ed.) *Amitav Ghosh*: 128-141.

—. 'Amitav Ghosh'. http://www.liteneyc.com

Times, London. 'Editorial on Opposition to the Ilbert Bill' 26 February 1883 in Barbara Harlow and Mia Carter (eds.) *Imperialism and Orientalism: A Documentary Sourcebook* Malden, Massachusetts: Blackwell, 1999: 220.

Tiwari, Shubha. *Amitav Ghosh: A Critical Study* New Delhi: Atlantic Publishers, 2003.

Todd, Tasmin. 'Malarial Dreams: Review of *The Calcutta Chromosome*'. *Washington Post Book World.* 27.50 (14 December 1997): 7.

Trikha, Pradeep. '*In An Antique Land*: A Traveller's Tale' in R.K. Dhawan (ed.) *The Novels of Amitav Ghosh.* New Delhi: Prestige, 1999: 187-91.

—. '*The Calcutta Chromosome*: A Literary Touchstone' in R.K. Dhawan (ed.) *The Novels of Amitav Ghosh* New Delhi: Prestige, 1999: 257-64.

Tripathi, Salil. 'The Past is Now: Review of *Dancing in Cambodia, At Large in Burma*'. *Far Eastern Economic Review.* 61.31 (30 July 1998): 42-43.

Trivedi, Darshana. 'Footprints of History' in Indira Bhatt and Indira Nityanandam (eds.) *The Fiction of Amitav Ghosh*: 142-49.

—. 'Here's God's Plenty' in Indira Bhatt and Indira Nityanandam (eds.) *The Fiction of Amitav Ghosh*: 34-39.

Veni, E. Kanaka Bhagya. 'The Image of Woman in *In An Antique Land*' in R. K. Dhawan (ed.) *The Novels of Amitav Ghosh*: 202-05.